Women

in

Ministry

by

Dr. George M. Stover Jr., D. Min., Th. D.

VISION PUBLISHING
Ramona, California

Vision Publishing
1115 D Street
Ramona, CA 92065
www.visionpublishingservices.com

Scriptures are taken from the King James Bible
and the Amplified Bible unless otherwise stated.

Dedicated to my dear wife

Dr. Sharon Stover, R. N., D. Min., Th. D., Ph. D.

Who has stayed faithful to her call in the face of all misunderstanding and opposition within, and without the Body of Christ.

And who has been such an encouragement during the long period of time needed to accumulate, analyze, assimilate, and assemble the material found in the following pages.

My heartfelt gratitude to

Patricia Rios

for her permission to use her work

"Forgiven"

on the cover and within the text of this book.
Also for her permission to use **"Nurtured,"**
"Adoration" and **"Covenant"** within these pages.

The works of Patricia Rios may be viewed and
purchased at the electronic bookstore of
Wellspring Ministries - Churches & Missions, Inc.

http://www.wellspringministries.com/bookst1.htm

or

http://www.smartcart.com/wellspring/index.cgi?page=welcome.htm

TABLE OF CONTENTS

CHAPTER I – BACKGROUND

Over the years I have been asked the same questions time and time again about the propriety of women preaching, teaching, leading and/or holding office in the church. I found that most of the questions stemmed from either a lack of teaching or concepts learned from various traditions that have firmly planted themselves in the fabric of church structure during the development of the various persuasions found in the Church of the Living God. The queries of some find their root in fears that women will take over if given too much authority, becoming unruly and unmanageable. Still others express the concern that women will lose their femininity, begin to lord it over their husbands, or worse yet, lead the church off into error because, after all, as some maintain, "the woman being deceived was in the transgression" (1 Tim. 2:14 KJV).[1] I began my Christian walk with what was once a typical male mind set that a woman's place was in the home. God began to deal with me concerning this traditional prejudice. I didn't know how it would work; I just knew that if the Lord was dealing with me I needed to allow Him to teach me, no matter what I thought. The result of His work in me has since enabled many capable and anointed women of God in our Church and around the world.

I have come to the conclusion that it is not only proper, but expedient that women be allowed to preach, teach, and lead in the church. Consider with me, if you will, the material that follows and see if you might not come to agree with my assessment.

The first book I ever read regarding women in ministry was Charles Trombley's book, <u>Who Said Women Can't Teach?</u> In it he observed the passion with which this subject has been discussed. In Chapter One he writes:

> The "woman" question isn't a simple issue. Instead, it is one of the most complex, emotional problems facing the Church. In March 1976, *Logos Journal* published an article about the Episcopalian debate, "Should Women Be Priests?" In 1983, Christianity Today devoted the best part of a whole issue to "Women At The Helm," paralleling the pros and cons of the ordination of women and the headship of men. Both sides of the issue were carefully represented but neither side solved the problem.

Is it scriptural for women to minister, and if not, why not? Who forbids them? Tradition, cultural and sexual bias, or masculine pride?[2]

My wife was licensed and ordained as a minister of the Gospel by our Pastor and friend Dr. William (Bill) Sharp in the year 1985. At present she co-pastors with me at Wellspring Church of All Nations. She is as godly, anointed and capable a person as I have ever met. Together we founded Wellspring Ministries - Churches & Missions, Inc., a church planting, missions training and sending organization. Her personal ministry extends around the world by means of books, audio and video tapes, and her personal travel to the nations.

Our working relationship has only deepened my regard for her. She is my lover, my wife, my prayer partner, my friend and my co-worker in this harvest field of Las Vegas, Nevada, and the world. I pray that this text will encourage others to enter into the joy that can be found when men and women learn to work together for the Lord.

I stand as one man who is tired of seeing women used as the brunt of jokes, being demeaned, degraded and their marvelous abilities being denigrated without cause. To me, any form of prejudice is unacceptable baggage in a Christian's life.

I am not setting forth a new concept, nor is modern feminism finding another advocate, but I am simply bringing to light liberating evidence that I believe is firmly established in the Scriptural record as well as the history of the Church. It is time that the Church of the Living God releases the potential of its female members and show the world how men and women should interact in every area of life. Whether a woman is married or not has absolutely no bearing on her ability to lead. The difference is simply whether or not she has a husband to relate to. I will touch more on this in Chapter VIII.

It is my observation that the women's liberation movement is not biblical nor is it the answer to the excessive subservience that women suffer in many cultures. Both men and women were to have dominion over the created order. This can be seen in Genesis 1:26-28:

> And God said, Let us make man in our image, after our likeness: and let them have dominion over the fish of the sea, and over the fowl of the air, and over the cattle, and over all

the earth, and over every creeping thing that creepeth upon the earth. So God created man in his own image, in the image of God created he him; male and female created he them. And God blessed them, and God said unto them, Be fruitful, and multiply, and replenish the earth, and subdue it: and have dominion over the fish of the sea, and over the fowl of the air, and over every living thing that moveth upon the earth. Genesis 1:26-28 (KJV)

The Hebrew word, אדם, 'adam, is the word used for a human being or mankind,[3] and the phrase "subdue it: and have dominion over" applies to fish, fowl of the air, and the animal kingdom, but does not allow for making human beings subservient or subject to one another. The concept here is that of shared authority under the leadership of the Almighty Himself. This categorizes any feminist movement as no more, and no less, than a female version of the male dominance that Jesus condemned at every opportunity. Jesus Christ came "to set at liberty them that are bruised" (Luke 4:18 KJV).

My wife and I have not reversed roles, nor have we tried to become what we are not. Each of us esteems the other higher than ourselves and therefore releases the other to become all that God has called us to become. As it is written, "Let nothing be done through strife or vainglory; but in lowliness of mind let each esteem the other better than themselves" (Phil. 2:3 KJV). This willingness to "each esteem the other better" is liberating to all who will embrace its simplicity and seek to deny their fleshly nature and follow Jesus as a humble servant who emancipates at every opportunity (Matt. 16:24 KJV).

In our liberty to follow the call of God on our lives, we are more readily able to encourage and strengthen each other along the way. Without the strife brought about by struggling for control, we find our energies available for creative and productive service to the King of kings and His priceless people.

You might ask, "Was it easy in the beginning?" Of course not. Working through the traditional thinking of our generation and moving into the fulness of God's call was not an easy task. But then, neither is learning to put off any of the other thought processes that we bring into our Christian life from the world. It was no more difficult than when any two leaders first join together to accomplish anything. Respect must be earned, strengths shared, weaknesses recognized and undergirded by the other, and dialogue, lots of it, must take place.

It would appear that the Apostle Paul felt that it would be even easier to fulfill God's call if one were single in that there could be a tendency to place one's spouse before the Lord, His plan and purpose:

But I would have you without carefulness. He that is unmarried careth for the things that belong to the Lord, how he may please the Lord: But he that is married careth for the things that are of the world, how he may please his wife. There is difference also between a wife and a virgin. The unmarried woman careth for the things of the Lord, that she may be holy both in body and in spirit: but she that is married careth for the things of the world, how she may please her husband. 1 Corinthians 7:32-34 (KJV)

Loren Cunningham is a man that I have met in various nations and at various times in my travels. He is a co-founder with his wife, Darlene, of Youth With A Mission, YWAM, an organization that has trained and released thousands of workers into the Lord's harvest field. Almost prophetically, Loren Cunningham declares in his newly released book, <u>Why Not Women</u>:

> This new generation will not be bound by traditions hindering women from obeying God's call the way my generation has . . . As this emerging generation studies the Bible free of cultural blinders, they will see that the Lord has always used both women and men to proclaim the Good News and to prophesy the Word of God to their generation.[4]

Over the years, I have encouraged many women to take their place in ministry and I, like Brother Loren, have found them to be a tremendous blessing. Many take their call seriously and serve the Lord with all of their being. There is a great army of willing and capable Christians who are waiting for someone to release them into the harvest fields of lost humanity. This army is not exclusively a man's army at all for it is open to all of the redeemed regardless of gender.

The admonition found in Matthew 28:19 and Mark 16:15 to go into all the world, preaching the gospel to every creature, teaching all nations, and baptizing them in the name of the Father, and of the Son, and of the Holy Ghost, is not a gender specific command. It is an all-inclusive command to every believer and is required of every Christian regardless of gender.

God has placed tremendous ability in mankind. Both men and women have talent, gifts, and graces that are only explained by the existence of a living, loving Creator. He is creative, and that creativity is seen in both men and women, His crowning creation. No one person, gender, race or nation has all of the abilities and giftings that have been bestowed upon mankind. The fulness of God's gracious gift is only found when all are allowed to contribute their supply of the Spirit. When we realize that two thirds of the world's Bible believing Christians are women, we must consider that if the women cannot preach, teach, or move in the things of the Spirit, that we are going to be greatly limited in our effectiveness of reaching the world.[5]

We are here challenged to receive the revelation that we are new creatures in Christ (2 Cor. 5:17; Gal. 6:15), and that old things have passed away and all things have become new (2 Cor. 5:17), and that we are the righteousness of God in Christ (2 Cor. 5:21). The walk of faith is learned as we hear the word of God. "So then faith cometh by hearing, and hearing by the word of God" (Rom. 10:17 KJV).

We hear, Paul "the Elder," encouraging a woman in ministry and doctrine as he penned the words preserved in 2 John 1:1, 5 and 9: "The Elder unto the elect lady." "And now I beseech thee, lady . . .". The word Κυρια, kuria, specifically refers to "a Christian woman."[6] It is obvious that this "elect lady" was active in the ministry and recognized by the Apostle.

We, as Christians, are to recognize that we are members one of another and members in particular of the body of Christ (1 Cor. 12:27). No one part has everything that the body needs:

For the body is not one member, but many. If the foot shall say, Because I am not the hand, I am not of the body; is it therefore not of the body? And if the ear shall say, Because I am not the eye, I am not of the body; is it therefore not of the body? If the whole body were an eye, where were the hearing? If the whole were hearing, where were the smelling? But now hath God set the members every one of them in the body, as it hath pleased him. And if they were all one member, where were the body? But now are they many members, yet but one body. And the eye cannot say unto the hand, I have no need of thee: nor again the head to the feet, I have no need of you. Nay, much more those members of the body, which seem to be more feeble, are necessary: And those members of the body, which we think to be less honourable, upon these we bestow more abundant honour; and our uncomely parts have more abundant comeliness. For our comely parts have no need: but God hath tempered the body together, having given more abundant honour to that part which lacked: That there should be no schism in the body; but that the members should have the same care one for another. 1 Corinthians 12:14-25 (KJV).

Simply put, we all need each other to become what God, in Christ, has called us to be. It is vitally necessary that every member of the body of Christ begin to become functional. Every part must fulfill its place. We must be careful that linear thinking does not cripple our effectiveness in spreading the gospel in this hour. We must come to realize that, "There is neither Jew nor Greek, there is neither bond nor free, there is neither male nor female . . ." (Gal. 3:28 KJV), for we all are now one in Christ.

God has made each one of us according to His

blue print. Not one of us has the same DNA, finger prints, eye scan, nor voice print. Each is a uniquely special creation, designed to fulfill a particular place in the Body of Christ. We are "members in particular" with a complete set of likes and dislikes, abilities and talents, outlooks and perspectives, plans and purposes, features and stature, as well as supernatural gifts of the Spirit designed to meet the needs of other Christians [the Church] and those that are in the world. All are endued with certain attributes that lend themselves to making the whole complete.

We should be aware that leadership ability is not found only in males. Many women have risen to a particular call and shown themselves extremely capable leaders. One of America's most outstanding statisticians, George Barna, defines a leader as follows:

> One who mobilizes; one whose focus is influencing people; a person who is goal driven; someone who has an orientation in common with those who rely upon him for leadership; and someone who has people willing to follow them.[7]

He also states that, "The Christlike Character of a Leader" is defined in terms such as:

A servant's heart, honesty, loyalty, perseverance, trustworthiness, courage, humility, sensitivity, teachability, values driven, optimistic, even tempered, joyful, gentle, consistent, spiritual depth, forgiving, compassionate, energetic, faithful, self-controlled, loving, wise, discerning, encouraging, passionate, fair, patient, kind, merciful, and reliable. Every one of these attributes can be found in both men and women who have allowed the character of Jesus to permeate their souls.

End of Chapter Questions
Chapter I

1. How open are you to concepts with which you may or may not agree?

2. Modern feminism has no bearing on whether a woman should be allowed to be a minister of the gospel.   True or False?

3. God told who to be fruitful and multiply?

4. The Hebrew word, אדם, 'adam, is the word used for_____ or _____.

5. When leaders join forces, respect must be _____, strengths _____, _____ recognized and undergirded.

6. The admonition found in Matthew 28:19 and Mark 16:15 to go into all the world, preaching the gospel to every creature is an all-_____ command.

7. What percent of the world's Bible believing Christians are women?

8. The Christ like character of a leader is defined in what terms?

CHAPTER II - AUTHORITY OF
SCRIPTURE

In order to find a solid foundation for our thinking we must agree upon an absolute authority; before which we will bow the knee of our existing concepts and yield to its decrees. We cannot give ear to the current trends of society, nor can we allow ourselves to be swayed by cultural bias when we seek truth. Trends, cultural preferences and contemporary philosophies change with the passage of time like the desert sand blown with the wind. Even modern science finds itself with uncertainties that only time and study will solidify. The arguments for an old earth verses a young earth are still, by some, hanging in the balance awaiting final analysis. Only one thing has proven itself again and again over the passing of time. Every finding in the sciences, including archeology, linguistics, genetics, quantum physics, and every other discipline, have done nothing but validate the authenticity and integrity of the Word of God. Our responsibility is to let the Word of God transform our nature and character into that of Christ, that is, to superimpose itself upon our whole being, rather than attempting to extrude the living Word to fit the shape of our concepts and traditions.

The Word of God is as unchanging as the God of the Word and is a sure anchor in the ever moving current of human thought. This great truth can be found in Matthew 24:35; Mark 13:31 and Luke 21:33. Each of these Scriptures presents the same theme: "Heaven and earth shall pass away, but my words shall not pass away." We can readily turn to the word of God and be reassured of its current validity for faith and practice. Therein we will see God still speaking, as we do in Malachi 3:6, "For I am the LORD, I change not." Now, let us allow the Teacher, the Holy Spirit, to instruct us by revealing truth in the word that He wrote and in 2 Timothy 3:16 declared to be "profitable for doctrine, for reproof, for correction, for instruction in righteousness."

As we move forward let us also allow that there are certain laws of interpretation that must be adhered to when confirming or establishing any doctrine. Some of these basic rules are referred to as: The Law of First Mention, Only Scripture may Interpret Scripture, Text Out of Context is Pretext, The Letter Kills, and The Spirit Gives Life.

Many well-meaning men and women misconstrue the intended meaning of certain passages due to ignorance resulting from a lack of educational background, inability to follow logic through to a reasonable conclusion, undisciplined thought process, or the inability or unwillingness to set aside learned tradition in the face of an accurate biblical exegesis. Unfortunately, the latter is the most prevalent. Tradition is the most difficult dragon to slay with the sword of the Spirit. So, let's begin at the beginning.

In the Book of Genesis we can allow the Law of First Mention, which allows that the Writer of the Word establishes the primary rule of understanding regarding any topic by His first mention of, and dealing with, the subject and/or topic, to take its proper place in our thinking. For instance, we see that in Genesis 1:26-28 (KJV) and Genesis 5:1-2 (KJV) the basis for our understanding that man and woman, together, were given the authority and command to, "Be fruitful, and multiply, and replenish the earth, and subdue it: and have dominion . . .". This understanding should anchor our thinking throughout the Scripture text whenever we consider authority issues.

And God said, Let us make man in our image,

after our likeness: and let them have dominion over the fish of the sea, and over the fowl of the air, and over the cattle, and over all the earth, and over every creeping thing that creepeth upon the earth. So God created man in his own image, in the image of God created he him; male and female created he them. And God blessed them, and God said unto them, Be fruitful, and multiply, and replenish the earth, and subdue it: and have dominion over the fish of the sea, and over the fowl of the air, and over every living thing that moveth upon the earth.

As mentioned previously, it is generally understood that the word "man," אדם, ʻadam, means a human being, mankind, male and/or female, and a person. This should be kept in mind as we consider the above verses. Adam was referred to as them. The name, Adam, originally referred to both male and female. They, both male and female, were to have dominion. They, both male and female, were blessed by God. They, both male and female, were told to be fruitful, and multiply, and replenish the earth, and subdue it: and have dominion. The word "dominion" is רדה, radah, and means "to rule, have dominion, dominate, tread down, rule, subjugate, to tread down, prevail against, reign, (bear, make to) rule, (-r, over), take."[8] Both men and women were established in this position of rulership.

The first order, before the fall, was established and equally given to both sexes without reservation or restriction. There was neither male nor female as is reiterated by Paul in the New Testament time and time again.

To strengthen the validity of the first mention of this theme God repeated the concept in the fifth chapter of Genesis, verses 1-2 (KJV): "This is the book of the generations of Adam. In the day that God created man, in the likeness of God made he him; Male and female created he them; and blessed them, and called their name Adam, in the day when they were created."

God explicitly states that both male and female were not only created by Him but were both created in His likeness. It was then reconfirmed that He blessed them both. The New Testament bears this out in the book of Galatians 3:28 (KJV), "There is neither Jew nor Greek, there is neither bond nor free, there is neither male nor female: for ye are all one in Christ Jesus" (emphasis mine).

God's original plan and design was that men and women be co-regents of the creation. This was lost during the fall but restored in Christ Jesus. Whether or not this has been fully realized by the average Christian is not at issue. This is the intent of God for our lives today. One was not designed to rule over the other. Each was to regard the wishes and thoughts of the other and they were to rule together. J. Lee Grady, in his book 10 Lies the Church Tells Women, said:

> Disagreements occur in Christian homes every day. In many cases, husbands and wives who argue over an issue will sit down, listen to each other, calmly try to understand the other spouse's perspective and then decide on a resolution. That's the way conflict management is supposed to work. But domestic strife can't be resolved if the husband believes (1) that he is always right, (2) that it is wrong for him to defer to his wife or (3) that his masculinity is weakened if he admits a mistake. If he believes all three of these fallacies, he qualifies as a first-degree tyrant.[9]

Both men and women are members of the Body of Christ. They both are also included in the picture of the Bride of Christ. This inclusivity shows us that there is no difference in the way God sees woman from the way He sees man. Man and woman are included in the Bride and both await their Bride-Groom, Jesus the Christ.

When Christ died we all died. When He arose from the dead, we all arose with Him. As it is written, both male and female believers are "buried with him in baptism, wherein also ye are risen with him through the faith of the operation of God, who hath raised him from the dead" (Col. 2:12 KJV). We are now seated at the right hand of God the Father in [and with] Christ and are to rule and reign with Him now while we learn how to rule and reign with Him for eternity:

> And what is the exceeding greatness of his power to us-ward who believe, according to the working of his mighty power, Which he wrought in Christ, when he raised him from the dead, and set him at his own right hand in the heavenly places, Far above all principality, and power, and might, and dominion, and every name that is named, not only in this world, but also in that which is to come: And hath put all things under his feet, and gave him to be the

head over all things to the church, Which is his body, the fulness of him that filleth all in all. And you hath he quickened, who were dead in trespasses and sins. Ephesians 1:19-2:1 (KJV)

As well as:

But God, who is rich in mercy, for his great love wherewith he loved us, Even when we were dead in sins, hath quickened us together with Christ, (by grace ye are saved;) And hath raised us up together, and made us sit together in heavenly places in Christ Jesus. Ephesians 2:4-6 (KJV)

This idea of co-rulership or co-regency is also seen in Dr. Fuschia Pickett's words, "Both man and woman are to walk together as one and let God fulfill the cry of their spirits for a true Bridegroom."[10] This concept is found in Genesis 2:24 where it reads, "Therefore shall a man leave his father and his mother, and shall cleave unto his wife: and they shall be one flesh." These same words are seen reinforced by the Lord in Matthew 19:5-6 and Mark 10:8 and are also quoted by the Apostle Paul in Ephesians 5:31. Doctor Pickett goes on to say, "The whole point is walking together as one."[11] We must agree with this line of thinking in that headship is not necessarily priesthood in the family unit, for we all are called to be royal priests.

It is proper that a man should take the lead in his family as it's head, but he should realize that the High Priest and Head of that "one flesh" family is Christ. This is at the heart of the original intent of God and the completion of the work of Christ as set forth in the Gospels: "And hath made us kings and priests unto God and his Father; to him be glory and dominion for ever and ever" (Rev. 1:6 KJV). "And hast made us unto our God kings and priests: and we shall reign on the earth" (Rev. 5:10 KJV). "Blessed and holy is he that hath part in the first resurrection: on such the second death hath no power, but they shall be priests of God and of Christ, and shall reign with him a thousand years" (Rev. 20:6 KJV).

We also have the same concept voiced in the words of Kelly Varner regarding the position of women as co-regents with men and with Christ Jesus: "Women can pray, proclaim, and learn. They are no longer under the shadow of Eve's deception any more than men are under the shadow of Adam's willful sin. Jesus redeemed the woman and the man from the curse."[12]

Every believer is called to live out this great truth in the light they have.

Adoniram Judson Gordon (1836 - 1895) was pastor of one of Boston's largest Baptist churches for over twenty-five years and, for the last seven years of his life, was also chairman of the American Baptist Missionary Union and Founder of a Bible school which has become Gordon College. He was also a hymn-writer and composer of hymn-tunes, an author of note, and a valued associate of D. L. Moody in his conference work. In an article penned circa 1890 called The Ministry of Women,[13] he set forth a scholarly, and convincing, observation concerning the classes of human beings being brought into equal privileges under the outpoured Holy Spirit. He believed that the dispensation of the Spirit ushered in the pristine economy which existed before the fall. Reverend Gordon used Acts 2:17-21, as well as, Romans 10:12, 13; 1 Corinthians 12:13; Galatians 3:28; Joel 2:28,29; and Acts 2:14-18 to support his arguments [see Appendix I].

He noted that Paul concluded all, irregardless of nationality, social status, or gender to be members of one body and insisted that the term "neither male nor female" is not in the least bit rhetorical, but that if the believing Gentile was ushered into the higher privileges that were found in God's outpouring of grace, then so did women. His reasoning was that both were spoken of in the same category, "There is neither Jew nor Greek, there is neither bond nor free, there is neither male nor female: for ye are all one in Christ Jesus" (Gal. 3:28 KJV).

The prophecy of Joel 2:28, 29, and restated in Acts 2:14-18, is seen by Reverend Gordon as the Magna Carta of the Christian Church and gives woman a status that had, prior to the Spirit's outpouring, never been known:

> And it shall come to pass afterward, that I will pour out my spirit upon all flesh; and your sons and your daughters shall prophesy, your old men shall dream dreams, your young men shall see visions: And also upon the servants and upon the handmaids in those days will I pour out my spirit. Joel 2:28-29 (KJV)

At the very least, these verses show that both male and female are recipients of His gifts and authorized to move in the power of them.

Positionally, both male and female believers are

seated in heavenly places with the sin nature dealt with, and the devil beneath their feet. That we have been made to sit together in heavenly places and that we have been blessed with all spiritual blessings, now, can be seen in verses such as Ephesians 1:3 and 2:6. "Blessed be the God and Father of our Lord Jesus Christ, who hath blessed us with all spiritual blessings in heavenly places in Christ" (Eph. 1:3 KJV). "And hath raised us up together, and made us sit together in heavenly places in Christ Jesus" (Eph. 2:6 KJV).

It would appear that we have clear, concise authority in the Word of God concerning the co-equal position, or status, of men and women in the context of Scripture. If this is true, then we have been withholding the rightful place of women in the Church for almost two thousand years.

"Nurtured" by Patricia Rios

End of Chapter Questions
Chapter II

1. What one thing has proven its authenticity and integrity in such a manner that we can safely bow the knee of our existing concepts and yield to its decrees?

2. Explain the "Law of First Mention" as it applies to interpreting the Scripture.

3. Define the biblical concept of co-regency.

4. Ephesians 2:6 shows, positionally, which believers are seated in the heavenly places with the sin nature dealt with, and the devil beneath their feet?

5. The rightful place of women in the church is what?

CHAPTER III - WOMEN IN MINISTRY

Perhaps now we should proceed to look at Biblical instances of women in ministry. As to the question of teaching, an apparent difficulty arises which seems, at first look, not easy to solve. If the Apostle Paul, in his words to Timothy, absolutely forbids a woman to teach and expound spiritual truth, especially to a man, then the remarkable instance of a woman doing this very thing is most disconcerting: "And he [Apollos] began to speak boldly in the synagogue: whom when Aquila and Priscilla had heard, they took him unto them, and expounded unto him the way of God more perfectly" (Acts 18:26 KJV). In light of this, some have held that the statement in 1 Timothy 2:9, with the entire paragraph to which it belongs, refers to the married woman's domestic relations, and not to her public relations, to her subjection to the teaching of her husband as against her ability and right to teach in public. This is the view of Canon Garratt, in his excellent observations on the ministry of women, as quoted in Times of Refreshing.

It may be said against the conclusion which we have reached concerning the position of women, that the plain reading of the New Testament makes a different impression on the mind. That may be so on two grounds; first on that of traditional bias; and second, on that of unfair translation.

Concerning the latter point, it would seem as though the translators of our common version wrought, at every point where this question occurs, under the shadow of Paul's imperative, Let your women keep silence in the churches. Let us take two illustrations from names found in that constellation of Christian women mentioned in Romans. "I commend unto you Phoebe our sister, which is a servant [minister, deacon] of the church which is at Cenchrea: That ye receive her in the Lord, as becometh saints, and that ye assist her in whatsoever business she hath need of you: for she hath been a succourer of many, and of myself also" (Rom. 16:1, 2). Not only is Phoebe a deacon, but we see that those to whom she was sent (both male and female) were to yield to her and were to stand ready to help in any way she might have need of. The word "servant" is the word diakonia, and it means "attendant (as a servant, etc.); figurative (eleemosynary) aid, (official) service (especially of the Christian teacher, or technical of the diaconate) :- (ad-) minister (-ing, -tration, -try), office, relief, service (-ing)." The church at Rome is told to "assist her." This word, "assist" is the Greek word *aristemi* which means, "stand beside, be at hand (or ready) to help, yield to; commend, substantiate, recommend."

The Amplified Bible accurately conveys this meaning:

Now I introduce and commend to you our sister Phoebe, a deaconess of the church at Cenchreae, That you may receive her in the Lord [with a Christian welcome], as saints (God's people) ought to receive one another. And help her in whatever matter she may require assistance from you, for she has been a helper of many including myself [shielding us from suffering]. Romans 16:1-2 (AMP).

The same word *diakonos*, here translated 'servant,' is rendered 'minister' when applied to Paul and Apollos in 1 Corinthians 3:5, and 'deacon' when used of other male officers of the Church (1 Tim. 3:10, 12, 13). Why discriminate against Phoebe simply because she is a woman? The word 'servant' is correct for the general unofficial use of the term, as in Matthew 22:10; but if Phoebe were really a functionary of the Church, we have a right to conclude, let her have the honor to which she is entitled. If 'Phoebe, a minister' of the Church at Cenchrea, sounds to bold, let the word be transliterated, and read, 'Phoebe, a deacon,' a deacon, indeed, without the insipid termination 'ess' of which there is no more need than that we should say teacheress or doctoress. It is wonderful how much there is in a name!

'Phoebe, a servant,' might suggest to an ordinary reader nothing more than the modern church helper, who prepares sandwiches and coffee for an ecclesiastical social."[14]

To Canon Garrett, with his genial and enlightened view of a woman's position in apostolic times, "Phoebe, a deacon," suggests a useful co-laborer with Paul, "traveling about on missionary and other labors of love." In the next two verses we see Paul greeting two of his "helpers in Christ Jesus" who risked their own lives to save his. His mention of the woman first "Greet Priscilla . . ." is notable considering that many have said that Paul was against women in ministry. Some have even gone so far as to call him "a woman hater." The normal greeting would have placed the husband first, but Paul apparently saw Priscilla as the leader in this ministry team.

This in no wise diminished his regard for Aquila who also laid down his life as he helped Paul, but showed his high regard for Priscilla as a minister as can be seen in the following verses: "Greet Priscilla and Aquila my helpers in Christ Jesus: Who have for my life laid down their own necks" (Acts 18:18 KJV). "And Paul after this tarried there yet a good while, and then took his leave of the brethren, and sailed thence into Syria, and with him Priscilla and Aquila" (Rom. 16:3-4). "Greet Priscilla and Aquila my helpers in Christ Jesus" (Rom. 16:3 KJV). The word "helpers" is συνεργος, sunergos.

According to the Strong's Exhaustive Concordance, sunergos is "from a presumed compound of Greek 4862 (sun) and the base of Greek 2041 (ergon); a co-laborer, i.e. coadjutor:- companion in labour, (fellow-) helper (-labourer, -worker), labourer together with, workfellow."[15] This Priscilla is one who is a "labourer together with" the Apostle. We also see in 2 Timothy 4:19 that Priscilla, or Prisca, is mentioned first: "Salute Prisca and Aquila." The majority of the original manuscripts places Priscilla before Aquila in the preceding verse of Acts 18:26 also. The Amplified Bible carries the more accurate rendering: "He began to speak freely (fearlessly and boldly) in the synagogue; but when Priscilla and Aquila heard him, they took him with them and expounded to him the way of God more definitely and accurately" (Acts 18:26 AMP). Again, it is worth mention that it was normal usage in the Greek language to place the husband before the wife. To depart from this grammatically correct rule was definitely a purposeful recognition of the stronger, or at least, more prominent ministry.

Clearly, here is a woman taking the lead as theological teacher to Apollos, an eminent minister of the Gospel, and so far setting up her authority as to tell him he is not thoroughly qualified for his work. This powerful statement was evidently overwhelming for the transcriber or critic who had final say over what word was to go where and he yielded to his tradition.

The Revised Version and the Amplified has rectified the error and the woman's name now leads.

What a beautiful story this is! How natural it seems to consider that, after listening to the Alexandrian orator Apollos, Priscilla would say to her husband: Yes, he is eloquent and mighty in the Scriptures, but can you imagine what he would be like if he were baptized in the Holy Spirit and fire? Can you imagine what he would be like if he were endued with power from on high? So they agreed that they would approach him and see if he were open to instruction. He was quite open, and more than willing, so they took him and instructed him concerning the Baptism with the Holy Ghost, with the result that he who before had been mighty in the Scriptures, now like never before, "mightily convinced the Jews."

> He began to speak freely (fearlessly and boldly) in the synagogue; but when Priscilla and Aquila heard him, they took him with them and expounded to him the way of God more definitely and accurately. And when he was disposed to pass into Achaia, the brethren wrote, exhorting the disciples to receive him: who, when he was come, helped them much which

had believed through grace: For he mightily convinced the Jews, and that publicly, showing by the scriptures that Jesus was Christ. Acts 18:26 (AMP)

It is evident that the Holy Spirit made this woman Priscilla a teacher of teachers as He has many women down through Church history.

D. L. Moody's preaching was forever transformed when Madam Guyon admonished him of his need of the secret of power and brought him under unspeakable obligation by teaching him of the Holy Spirit baptism, just as many a man of God was changed when Katheryn Kuhlman introduced them to the Person of the Holy Spirit.

We find Charles L. Thompson, D.D., saying the following regarding women in ministry:[16]

Should women converse only with women? Not at all. It is, perhaps, most natural that ordinarily this should be the case. But there are many circumstances which would render it desirable that women should converse with anxious men ("anxious men" refer to those who are experiencing the convicting power of the Holy Ghost after hearing the Gospel preached).

There are conditions, even of intellectual difficulty, which may best be met by intelligent women. Within the past few months a case in point came under our observation. A young skeptic of remarkable intelligence, and some pride of skeptical opinion, had been successively conversed with by many evangelists, pastors, and others.

He was evidently somewhat impressed with the need of spiritual life and help; every attempt to bring him face to face with Christ he would ward off by propounding difficult questions in speculative theology. Every appeal was met either by argument or by some cynical remark which neutralized its effect. At length, one evening the leader of the inquiry meeting introduced Mr. A. to a Christian woman. His first remark was, "So you have come to interview me." The reply was, "No, I do not know enough for that. I want you to interview me, or rather let us both interview the Bible and see what we can learn."

Somewhat disarmed by this reply, his tone changed, and he expressed himself very willing to have a conversation. But his old habit returning upon him, he propounded one after another of the intellectual difficulties in his way.

The lady met each one by saying, "I cannot answer you. I will not pretend to; but let us see what God says about it;" and then opening the Bible she would read such passages as gave a Divine answer to the inquiry. In this way he was pressed by the sword of the Spirit from point to point, until unable longer to continue the struggle, he sprang to his feet exclaiming, "This question must be settled tonight. Pray for me!" The result was his conversion – not as the result of the argument he coveted – but of a judicious use of Divine truth. Instances of this sort might be indefinitely multiplied. They prove that the superior conversational powers of women have found a field new and wide, and telling upon the highest of human interests. Henceforth, can it be doubted, the qualities of mind and heart that have made so many parlors sources of great social influence, will be more freely used in commending to society the grand themes and the blessed hopes of the Christian religion?

Further in the same book the author notes that:

Men set the key of debates and lectures, but women give the pitch of conversation. . . . If ennobling, to them belongs the honor. . . . It is in the power of women to regenerate society, lift it out of vapidity and gossip into the noblest realm of human thought, by daring to make Christian faith, life, and hope, a free and open subject of parlor talk. The world is to be converted, not by the stately artillery that is reserved for intellectual battles, but by the impact of heart on heart in office and shop and parlor and kitchen. In this personal address women are peerless. Let them use their fine intuitions and their ready art of apt and feeling speech for the kingdom of Christ, and they may do more for the spread of that kingdom than Mercurius, by his dialectic skill or Boanerges, by his resounding eloquence.[17]

These profound insights out of the past reveal both the struggle of women to be heard and the great influence they had when allowed to express themselves concerning the Gospel.

Fortunately, in every age, there have been men

who are not threatened by their involvement nor are willing to suppress them based upon gender prejudice that cannot be upheld but by twisting the Holy Word.

We will consider the favorite "proof text" of 1 Timothy 2:9, forbidding women the right to teach or preach, in detail on pages 67 - 76 as well as other often misunderstood texts.

"Adoration" by Patricia Rios

End of Chapter Questions
Chapter III

1. The Greek word *diakonia* may be understood by what four definitions?
2. *Aristemi* is understood to mean what?
3. Priscilla, the wife of Aquila, was used by the Holy Spirit to teach what eminent minister of the gospel?
4. Who said, "Men set the key of debates and lectures, but women give the pitch of conversation?"
5. Do you agree or disagree with the statement in question 4 above? Explain why.

CHAPTER IV - PAUL'S VIEW OF WOMEN

Although there have been those who say that Paul was a woman hater, the truth was quite the opposite. There is no doubt that Paul was very aware of and thankful for women who labored in the work of the Lord. "Salute Tryphena and Tryphosa, who labour in the Lord. Salute the beloved Persis, which laboured much in the Lord" (Rom. 16:12 KJV).

What was the "labour" in the Lord these women were so appreciated by Paul for? Put this quotation together with that of Philippians 4:3: "Help those women which labored with me in the Gospel." Did they labor in the Lord under some kind of secret oath to never give public witness to the Lord? There is no such implication! No, it would seem that they labored in the Gospel just like the men did.

Now, what of the word of Paul to Timothy as found in 1 Timothy 2:11, "Let the women learn in silence?" I submit that there is traditional prejudice bringing out an insidiously misleading translation that gives rise to the following remarks: "Should the church have women preachers? No. That's exactly what the verse forbids. In the public service, women are not to teach. They are responsible to teach other women only."[18]

John MacArthur, in his book, The Masters Plan for the Church, contradicts his statement that women should only teach other women when he says that it is a given that women should teach their children, some of whom are male. While many would not argue that women should teach their sons, it would seem schizophrenic to allow them input into the young males when they are so impressionable and open to new ideas, and yet not allow them to give input when they are mature and established in their development.

Rightly, the Amplified Bible, along with several other respected versions including the New International Version [NIV], the New American Standard Bible [NASB], and the New Jerusalem Bible [NJB] vindicates the purity of Scripture and renders the word ησυχια, hesuchia, as quietness.

The Thayer's Greek Lexicon so reads: "Greek 2271, Strong's hesuchia, *hay-soo-khee'-ah*; feminine of Greek 2272 (hesuchios); (as noun) *stillness*, i.e. desistance from bustle or language :- *quietness*, silence."[19] Although The Message Bible is not considered an exceptionally scholarly rendition of the

Scripture, I believe it offers an understandable example of this concept in 1 Timothy 2:11. "During instruction, a woman should be quiet and respectful."[20] The Amplified Bible renders the verse: "Let a woman learn in quietness . . ." This word "quietness," meaning quiet and respectful, is in complete harmony with the idea of proper witness, prayer, and prophesy in the Christian assembly. It should be noted that when men are admonished along the same line the word ησυχια, hesuchia, is also translated quietness: "That with quietness they work and eat their own bread" (2 Thess. 3:12 KJV), an injunction which no reader would construe to mean that they should refrain from speaking while working or eating.

Paul also encouraged those that were married to travel with their wives and to treat them with great respect and love:

> Have we not power to lead about a sister, a wife, as well as other apostles, and as the brethren of the Lord, and Cephas (1 Corinthians 9:5 KJV)?

> So ought men to love their wives as their own bodies. He that loveth his wife loveth himself (Ephesians 5:28 KJV).

-45-

For this cause shall a man leave his father and mother, and shall be joined unto his wife, and they two shall be one flesh (Ephesians 5:31 KJV).

These are the words of anyone but a man who has no use for women. Paul was a man who worked with them, cherished them, and respected them as they labored together with the apostles and disciples of the Lord. This, I believe, will become more and more obvious as we look at the next chapter.

End of Chapter Questions
Chapter IV

1. What would you respond to someone who believes that Paul was a woman hater?
2. Understanding the meaning of *hesuchia* is critical to understand 1 Timothy 2:11. Define the word.
3. Give three verses that show Paul's regard for women.

CHAPTER V - MISUNDERSTOOD TEXTS

The Apostle Peter said of Paul's writings that there were "some things hard to be understood, which they that are unlearned and unstable wrest, as they do also the other scriptures, unto their own destruction" (2 Pet. 3:16 KJV). It should not surprise us, then, to find that there are certain texts which are a matter of controversy and are often misunderstood.

Allow me to begin with 1 Corinthians11:2-16:

> Now I praise you, brethren, that ye remember me in all things, and keep the ordinances, as I delivered them to you. But I would have you know, that the head of every man is Christ; and the head of the woman is the man; and the head of Christ is God. Every man praying or prophesying, having his head covered, dishonoureth his head. But every woman that prayeth or prophesieth with her head uncovered dishonoureth her head: for that is even all one as if she were shaven. For if the woman be not covered, let her also be shorn: but if it be a shame for a woman to be shorn or

shaven, let her be covered. For a man indeed ought not to cover his head, forasmuch as he is the image and glory of God: but the woman is the glory of the man. For the man is not of the woman; but the woman of the man. Neither was the man created for the woman; but the woman for the man.

For this cause ought the woman to have power on her head because of the angels. Nevertheless neither is the man without the woman, neither the woman without the man, in the Lord. For as the woman is of the man, even so is the man also by the woman; but all things of God. Judge in yourselves: is it comely that a woman pray unto God uncovered? Doth not even nature itself teach you, that, if a man have long hair, it is a shame unto him? But if a woman have long hair, it is a glory to her: for her hair is given her for a covering. But if any man seem to be contentious, we have no such custom, neither the churches of God (KJV).

This passage of Scripture focuses primarily on proper attitudes and conduct in worship, not on the marriage relationship or on the role of women in the church as some believe. While Paul's specific instructions may be cultural (women covering their heads in worship), the principles behind his specific instructions are timeless, principles like respect for spouse, reverence and appropriateness in worship, and focus of all of life on God. The principle is this; if anything you do can easily offend members and divide the church, then change your ways to promote church unity. This is why Paul told the women who were not wearing head coverings to wear them, not because it was a Scriptural command, but because it kept the congregation from dividing over a petty issue that served only to take people's minds off Christ.

Granted, there are still those who maintain that women should be covered or, at least, should find ways that are "culturally appropriate ways for women to show respect for their husbands."[21] Their interpretations of what is proper covering runs the gamut from wearing scarves or hats to, as one church in Las Vegas demands, pink hair comb clips to show that they are "under submission" to their leadership.

As we look at 1 Corinthians 11:2, we need to read it in the context of the situation in Corinth realizing that Paul's main concern is not head covering but rather irreverence in worship. Karen Adlong wrote an article called, <u>Women of Faith the Real World Changers</u> and proffered the following observation:

> The matter of wearing hats or head coverings, although seemingly insignificant, had become a big problem because two cultural backgrounds were colliding. Jewish women always covered their heads in worship. For a woman to uncover her head in public was a sign of loose morals.[22]

On the other hand, Greek women may have been used to worshiping without head coverings. In this letter Paul had already spoken about divisions and disorder in the church. Both are involved in this issue. Paul's solution comes from his desire for unity among church members and for appropriateness in the worship service. He accepted God's sovereignty in creating the rules for relationships. "But I would have you know, that the head of every man is Christ; and the head of the woman *is* the man; and the head of Christ *is* God" (1 Cor. 11:3 KJV). The word head, κεφαλη, <u>kephale</u>, was a Gnostic term for source in Paul's day. The word head never meant final authority, decision maker or superior in rank. Paul was speaking to the Greek converts to Christianity and would have used an entirely different Greek word if he had wanted to convey the idea of ruler or leader.

Before the fall in the Garden of Eden both Adam and Eve had equal authority, position and dominion. She was, however, taken from Adam's side. He, therefore was her source, her kephale. The word αρχων, archon, [chief, magistrate, or chief ruler], which is used of "a certain ruler" in Matthew 9:18, could have been used rather than kephale, as could the word προιστημι, proistemi [to superintend, to preside over, to be guardian of], found in Romans 12:8, or ηγεομαι, hegeomai [to lead, command (with official authority), have the rule over] as found in Hebrews 13:17, where Christians were told to obey those that had rule over them. Therefore, Κεφαλη, kephale was chosen and is seen to mean the same as it does in Ephesians 5:23 where it refers to the husband as the source of the wife, even as Christ is the Source of the church, and in Colossians 1:18 where we see Christ referred to as the Source of the body, the beginning, and the firstborn.

The issue at hand is at once cultural and timeless. The issue of head covering [hats, veils, etc.]

was cultural, while the main point is that of properly honoring God by properly honoring the family institution. Therefore, the only conclusion we can make here is that Christ was, and is due to His eternal nature, the Source of every [all, any, every] man. Adam was the source of Eve. The Source of The Anointed One was God. The Source of the Anointing of the Anointed One is God.

For a male to pray or prophesy having his head covered would imply to the early Jewish convert to Christianity that he was still living under the law and not under the matchless grace of Christ. It is with this understanding that 1 Corinthians 11:4 (KJV) maintains its clarity. "Every man praying or prophesying, having *his* head covered, dishonoureth his head." It is helpful to understand that the word man is the Greek word ανερ, aner, which means an individual male. Kephale, or head, means source, while covered is κατα, kata, and means held down; in opposition, against; and dishonoreth is καταισχυνω, kataischuno, and means to shame, dishonor, treat shamefully, disgrace, or make blush.[23] The passage could then be understood to say, Every male praying or prophesying, and not recognizing the Lord as the source of all things, treats

Him shamefully, dishonors, and disgraces Him.

As we read the next verse, 1 Corinthians 11:5, "But every woman that prayeth or prophesieth with *her* head uncovered dishonoureth her head: for that is even all one as if she were shaven" (KJV), we must also understand the Greek words used in the text. Again, we turn to Dr. Alfred Edersheim as he notes that the Greek word γυνη gune, translated woman, means especially a wife. The word head is the same as in verse four as is the word dishonoreth. A woman accused of adultery was to have her hair shorn or shaven.[24] To pray, then, with head uncovered and culturally disgrace her husband by appearing to be a woman accused of adultery, would dishonor her husband, or source. The verse could also be understood to mean that she was praying in opposition to, or against, her husband. Either rendering would be totally unacceptable behavior on her part.

So, if she is unwilling to dress and act appropriately culturally, then she should be marked as a rebel to established order. A married woman should dress and act becomingly so as to bring honor to her husband and, especially, to Christ. "For if the woman be not covered, let her also be shorn: but if it be a shame for a woman to be shorn or shaven, let her be covered" (1 Cor. 11:6 KJV). This same principle would be good advice for how husbands present themselves in public also. "For a man indeed ought not to cover *his* head, forasmuch as he is the image and glory of God: but the woman is the glory of the man" (1 Cor. 11:7 KJV). A man, then, is to manifest Christ likeness in all that he does and should never hide the fact that he is a member of God's family. So, in like manner, the wife should always bring honor to her husband by her demeanor.

1 Corinthians 11:8, 9 (KJV) simply tells us that the source, κεφαλη, <u>kephale</u>, of the woman is the man, not the man of the woman. "For the man is not of the woman; but the woman of the man. Neither was the man created for the woman; but the woman for the man."

Now, what in the world is 1 Corinthians 11:10 talking about? What do angels have to do with the dress code of the culture? The King James Version reads, "For this cause ought the woman to have power on *her* head because of the angels." The word power is εξουσια, <u>exousia</u>, and is understood to mean: power of choice, the power of rule or government (the power of him whose will and commands must be submitted to by others and obeyed), liberty of doing as one pleases, the power of authority (influence) and of right (privilege), privilege due to ability, competency, and, therefore, freedom.[25] The idea of power on her head is that of having the noticeable confidence and delegated authority of her husband. This, as mentioned earlier, was conveyed culturally by the wearing of a veil by believing Jewish women, although not by the Greek believers. The term because of the angels is δια αγγελος, dia aggelos, which can be accurately translated "for the sake of the Pastors [messengers, Apostles, etc.]."[26] This greatly clears up the question of what is being set forth. It simply states that the Apostle Paul could easily recognize a woman of character by her dress and demeanor. My Pastor, Dr. Bill Sharp, used to speak of a modern version of this same thought. It went something like this: If every prostitute in Las Vegas, Nevada, carried a red purse to inform her potential clients that she was available for hire, then it would not be a good witness for a Christian lady to carry around a red purse. Can we understand the practicality of such an example?

These next two verses deal with the fact that the

Lord does not show any partiality between men and women. "Nevertheless neither is the man without the woman, neither the woman without the man, in the Lord. For as the woman *is* of the man, even so *is* the man also by the woman; but all things of God" (1 Cor. 11:11-12 KJV). This is a reminder that men and women have their ultimate source in God. The original woman was taken out of man but, from then on man comes out of, is born of, the woman. The equality of men and women, husbands and wives specifically, is reinforced here. There is an interdependence, an equal need for the other, in the design of God who is our Source, Κεφαλη, Kephale; one is not without the other.

"Judge in yourselves: is it comely that a woman pray unto God uncovered?" (1 Cor. 11:13 KJV). Here the cultural question of traditional propriety is thrown open for a Godly ruling. I would suggest that before you make a determination perhaps you might want to read the rule of the Law for a Nazarite in Numbers 6:1, 5, where the men, as well as the women, were commanded to not cut their hair:

> And the Lord spake unto Moses, saying, Speak unto the children of Israel, and say unto them, When either man or woman shall separate

themselves to vow a vow of a Nazarite, to separate themselves unto the Lord: (v.1) . . . All the days of the vow of his separation there shall no razor come upon his head: until the days be fulfilled, in the which he separateth himself unto the Lord, he shall be holy, and shall let the locks of the hair of his head grow. (v.5)

1 Corinthians 11:14 (KJV) carries the "We've always done it this way" idea. "Doth not even nature itself teach you, that, if a man have long hair, it is a shame unto him?" The word nature here is the Greek word φυσις, phusis, and holds the sense of native disposition or common usage. It is the traditional stance of a culture taught to do things a certain way.

"But if any man seem to be contentious, we have no such custom, neither the churches of God" (1 Cor. 11:16 KJV). This is the conclusion of the argument: No such custom! The whole point of dealing with the subject of covering was to show that Jesus rent the veil of the Holy of Holies and that both male and female could now come to God uncovered [with open face]:

Jesus, when he had cried again with a loud voice, yielded up the ghost. And, behold, the veil of the temple was rent in twain from the top to the bottom; and the earth did quake, and the rocks rent. Matthew 27:50-51 (KJV)

And the veil of the temple was rent in twain from the top to the bottom. Mark 15:38 (KJV)

And the sun was darkened, and the veil of the temple was rent in the midst. Luke 23:45 (KJV)

Wherein God, willing more abundantly to shew unto the heirs of promise the immutability of his counsel, confirmed it by an oath: That by two immutable things, in which it was impossible for God to lie, we might have a strong consolation, who have fled for refuge to lay hold upon the hope set before us: Which hope we have as an anchor of the soul, both sure and stedfast, and which entereth into that within the veil; Whither the forerunner is for us entered, even Jesus, made an high priest for ever after the order of Melchisedec. Hebrews 6:17-20 (KJV).

Having therefore, brethren, boldness to enter into the holiest by the blood of Jesus, By a new and living way, which he hath consecrated for us, through the veil, that is to say, his flesh; And having an high priest over the house of God; Let us draw near with a true heart in full assurance of faith, having our hearts sprinkled from an evil conscience, and our bodies washed with pure water. Hebrews 10:19-22 (KJV)

1 Timothy 2:12-14 (KJV) is a passage that many have used to declare that women cannot teach men. At a casual glance that may seem correct, but let's take a closer look:

But I suffer not a woman to teach, nor to usurp authority over the man, but to be in silence. For Adam was first formed, then Eve. And Adam was not deceived, but the woman being deceived was in the transgression.

The context in which we find these verses is that of Paul teaching about prayer. He wants men and women to pray and tells them how. We can see him specifically including the women in 1 Timothy 2:9 where he writes, "In like manner also." Both men and women are to pray every where without wrath and doubting and with holy hands lifted in praise to God.

An interesting point has been made by J. Lee Grady in his work, 10 Lies the Church Tells Women, where he states that these verses were in answer to the gnostic teaching of that time. Eve had been elevated to divinity as the "illuminator," and believed that she brought spiritual liberation to creation by eating the forbidden fruit in the garden. He notes that these heretics taught that she became Adam's mother rather than his wife and that she should be seen as the progenitor of all mankind. "These cultists worshiped the female deity known as Artemus, also known as Diana." It was this heresy that Paul was warning Timothy about and this was the reason that he set forth the creation story in no uncertain terms. [27]

Also worthy of our consideration is the fact that Paul was speaking to the church in which Priscilla had been a founding leader and where she and her husband, Aquila, had spent a great deal of time correcting the early errors of Apollos while discipling him for greater leadership in the Church. It was this same Paul who had asked the church in Rome to receive Phoebe with respect and honor. It hardly seems logical that Paul would now contradict himself and forbid Timothy to allow women to be teachers and leaders in the Church. By looking at the grammatical structure of these verses and those surrounding them we find that Paul apparently had moved from speaking to women in general to a particular woman who was teaching error. He then resumed speaking concerning all women. There is no suggestion here that all women must be silent [quiet] in all circumstances, nor is it a blanket statement forbidding women to teach and lead. We should also consider that the word used for woman in these verses is γυνη, gune, which specifically means a wife, while the word used for man is a word that is typically used for husband, ανερ, aner. It is most likely that Paul was speaking of a specific married woman and her relationship with her own husband.

It would be appropriate here to include some thoughts of the wonderful scholar, Dr. Fuschia Pickett:

> There was nothing to which Jesus laid the ax more violently than the traditions of men. Because of bondage to tradition, some cannot understand that there is no difference between male and female, for they have not come to faith. Paul declared that when we come to faith we will understand that there is neither Greek or Barbarian, nor male or female, but we are all one in Christ Jesus. God is preparing men and women alike to be filled with His Spirit in the

fullness of time, and is delivering us from tradition, prejudice, culture, and denominationalism.

We have tried to lay a guilt trip on men by telling them they are to fulfill every desire and deepest need of a woman. Men have been put in bondage by the expectation of their wives to meet every need of their lives. Though husbands should meet the physical and emotional needs of their wives, they cannot be expected to meet their spiritual needs. That is not God's divine order. Both man and woman are to walk together as one and let God fulfill the cry of their spirits for a true Bridegroom.

Many men have been gloriously delivered from the burden that some marriage counselors put upon them to meet their wife's every need. That was not God's intention. God ordained that men and woman should walk with Him and be as one, and He would meet the innermost needs of both of them. Divine order is higher than the plight of fallen man. It is far more liberating to men and women than having to live under the doctrine of the curse of a fallen Adam and a fallen Eve.

We have been redeemed to be one flesh in Him, bought with a price so that husbands and wives can truly become one. Paul admonishes us: "Submitting yourselves one to another in the fear of God. Wives, submit yourselves unto your own husbands, as unto the Lord. For the husband is the head of the wife, even as Christ is the head of the church: and he is the saviour of the body. Therefore as the church is subject unto Christ, so let the wives be to their own husbands in every thing" (Eph. 5:21-24 KJV).[28]

Whosoever will, Jew and Greek, bond and free, male and female, have bold access to the throne of grace. It is each believer's privilege to cry, "Abba, Father." This is every male and female believer's great privilege and joy. As we read in Romans 8:15, "For ye have not received the spirit of bondage again to fear; but ye have received the Spirit of adoption, whereby we cry, Abba, Father." This is reinforced by Hebrews 4:16 where it encourages all to "come boldly unto the throne of grace, that we may obtain mercy, and find grace to help in time of need."

To help further clarify the above I offer the most

easily understood modern language interpretation of 1 Corinthians 11:3-16 available today. This is found in The Message New Testament. The reading of it here will add much to a clear understanding of the original intent of the Scripture text:

In a marriage relationship, there is authority from Christ to husband, and from husband to wife. The authority of Christ is the authority of God. Any man who speaks with God or about God in a way that shows a lack of respect for the authority of Christ, dishonors Christ. In the same way, a wife who speaks with God in a way that shows a lack of respect for the authority of her husband, dishonors her husband. Worse, she dishonors herself - an ugly sight, like a woman with her head shaved.

This is basically the origin of these customs we have of women wearing head coverings in worship, while men take their hats off. By these symbolic acts, men and women, who far too often butt heads with each other, submit their heads to the Head; the Almighty Himself. Don't, by the way, read too much into the differences here between men and women.

Neither man nor woman can go it alone or claim priority. Man was created first, as a beautiful shining reflection of God—that is true. But the head on a woman's body clearly outshines in beauty the head of her head, her husband. The first woman came from man, true - but ever since then, every man comes from a woman! And since virtually everything comes from God anyway, let's quit going through these who's first routines. Don't you agree there is something naturally powerful in the symbolism - woman, her beautiful hair reminiscent of angels, praying in adoration; a man, his head bared in reverence, praying in submission? I hope you're not going to be argumentative about this. All God's churches see it this way; I don't want you standing out as an exception.

The passage of Scripture found in 1 Timothy 2:8 -11 has been wielded as the strongest and most decisive proof that women should be silent in the Church. It would, most likely, startle many proponents of this line of thinking were it shown that it really contains an exhortation to ordered and proper participation of women in public prayer. Such is the conclusion of some of the best exegetes. This makes it one of the most crucial of texts for us to understand properly.

I will therefore that men pray every where, lifting up holy hands, without wrath and doubting. In like manner also, that women adorn themselves in modest apparel, with shamefacedness and sobriety; not with broided hair, or gold, or pearls, or costly array; But (which becometh women professing godliness) with good works. Let the woman learn in silence with all subjection. 1 Timothy 2:8-11 (KJV)

By general consent, the force of the word βουλομαι, boulomai, "I will," is carried over from the eighth verse into the ninth: "I will that women . . ." This word carries the meaning, to will deliberately, have a purpose, be of a particular mind. What exactly is it that the apostle will have women do? The word ωσαυτως, hosautos, "in like manner," gives us a very substantial hint toward one answer, and a very substantial hindrance to another, and more common, answer.

We should ask if Paul meant that he would have the men pray in every place and the women, in like manner, to be silent. It doesn't seem likely does it?

Where would be the similarity of conduct that is called for in the two instances? Or, does the intended likeness lie between the men's lifting up holy hands, and the women's adorning themselves in modest apparel? Hardly likely. So unlikely, in fact, is either of these conclusions from the Apostle's language, that John Chrysostom (337-407), Bishop of Constantinople, and most commentators supply, "to pray," in order to complete the sense.

If they are right in so interpreting the intent of the passage, and I believe the word ωσαυτως, hosautos, (in like manner), compels them to do so, then the meaning is unquestionable. It should be understood as: "I will therefore that men pray everywhere, lifting up holy hands, etc. In like manner I will that women pray in modest apparel, etc."

In one of the most discerning and clearly reasoned pieces of exegesis by Peter Wiesinger, an eminent and learned commentator of the late seventeenth century [1899], we find his completely justified interpretation outlined below:

1. In the words 'in every place' it is chiefly to be observed that it is public prayer and not secret prayer that is spoken of.

2.   The word *proseuchesthai*, 'to pray' is to be
        supplied in verse 9, and to be connected with 'in
        modest apparel,' so that this special injunction
        as to the conduct of women in prayer
        corresponds to that given to the men in the word
        'Lifting up holy hands.' This verse, then, from
        the beginning, refers to prayer; and what is said
        of the women in verses 9 and 10 is to be
        understood as referring primarily to public
        prayer.

3.   The transition in verse 11 from *gunaikes* to *gune*
        shows that the apostle now passes on to
        something new. He is now speaking of the
        relation of the married woman to her husband
        (in the public assembly). She is to be in
        quietness rather than drawing attention to
        herself by public appearance, to learn rather
        than to teach, to be in subjection rather than in
        authority. There is no evidence from this
        passage that women were forbidden to pray in
        the public assembles of the Church. One might
        consider that they have been advised to refrain
        from public teaching. This latter question will
        be considered further on in the text."

Every man praying or prophesying, having *his* head covered, dishonoureth his head. But every woman that prayeth or prophesieth with *her* head uncovered dishonoureth her head: for that is even all one as if she were shaven. 1 Corinthians 11:4-5 (KJV).[29]

As we consider this verse in regard to public worship and the proper exercise of it, we see instruction given first to the man and then to the woman: "Every man praying or prophesying" and then, "Every woman praying or prophesying." An early commentary records this terse comment: Therefore women were not excluded from these duties.

Consider this, would the apostle take the time to prune a custom which he desired to uproot. Would he waste his breath condemning what many believe to be a forbidden method of doing a forbidden thing? The passage above is strikingly like the one considered prior to it, in that the proper order of doing is prescribed for the man and the woman. It does not seem reasonable to conclude that the thing considered would then be encouraged for the one and forbidden to the other. If the "in like manner" has raised a barrier to finding an injunction for the silence of women in prayer so too this passage expands her right to public prayer to include prophesying in public also.

Next, let's look at what many consider to be a decisive proof text in the quest to silence women in the public assembly. "Let your women keep silence in the churches: for it is not permitted unto them to speak; but they are commanded to be under obedience, as also saith the law. And if they will learn any thing, let them ask their husbands at home: for it is a shame for women to speak in the church" (1 Cor. 14:34, 35). To rightly understand the apostle's teaching we must here again consider the conduct of women in the Church as it relates to that of men. The injunction to silence, σιαγω, sigao, is used three times in 1 Corinthians 14; twice for men and once for women. The silence in each case is conditional, not absolute. I return, again, to Peter Wiesinger's excellent exegetical outline:

1. In verse 28, "Let him keep silence in the church," is said to one speaking with tongues, but on the condition that there be no interpreter.

2. In verse 30, "Let the first keep silence," it is said of those prophesying that they should speak two or three, but on the condition that it be revealed to another that is sitting nearby.

3. "Let your women keep silence in the churches" it is said again, but it is evidently on condition of their interrupting the service with questions, since it is added, "for it is not permitted them to speak . . . and if they will learn any thing, let them ask their husbands at home." This last clause takes the injunction clearly out of all reference to praying or prophesying, and shows what the whole chapter indicates, that the apostle is here dealing with the various forms of disorder and confusion prevalent in the church at that time.

4. He is not repressing the proper exercise of spiritual gifts, either by men or by women. If he were forbidding women to pray or prophesy in public, as some argue, what could be more irrelevant or meaningless than his directive concerning the case in point: if they will learn any thing, let them ask their husbands at home?

    It would be good to note here that these verses cannot be applied to all women, but only to those that are married and with their husbands.[30]

    Also, it should be considered that the synagogues of New Testament record had separate antechambers for the women. I have visited the historical sites of Israel and seen these separate compartments where women were seated. They were not permitted to sit with their husbands and so would disrupt the services if they were allowed to clarify what was being said by asking their husbands during the ministration of the speaker.

The clear conclusion is that there is nothing in the previous texts that would limit the public ministry of women who are of good character. Every passage of Scripture must be considered in the light of context and intent as taught in the New Testament. It's teaching conveys a three fold cord of the teaching of prophecy, the teaching of practice, and the teaching of contemporary history. Herein is found the true meaning of the Word of God as it sheds it's liberating light on the society and culture of our time.

This whole question can be summed up by considering the Scriptural record of the ministry of gifts in the earliest days of Christianity. Those were times of glorious and sanctified spiritual freedom that show and justify the custom of public ministration by women at that time in the Church.

The very ground and title of this ministry being

the acknowledged possession of gifts being bestowed on women as well as men.

Both the former and the latter were allowed to use them in Christian Assemblies. This seems to me quite evident from Paul's words in 1 Corinthians 11:5 where he strongly condemns the practice of women praying or prophesying with head unveiled, without expressing the least objection to this public ministration on their part, but only finding fault with what was at that time considered to be unseemly attire for women who were publicly engaged in such ministry. The injunction contained in the same epistle, found in 1 Corinthians 14:34 (KJV), "Let your women keep silence," etc. refers, as the context shows, not to prophesying or praying in the congregation, but to making remarks and asking questions about the words of others.

We may conclude without overconfidence, that on the whole, there is no Scripture prohibiting women from praying or prophesying in the public assemblies of the Church. On the contrary, it seems that in Acts 2:17 (KJV) they are being exhorted to prophesy: "And it shall come to pass in the last days, saith God, I will pour out of my Spirit upon all flesh: and your sons and your daughters shall prophesy, . . ." It appears that women have a threefold warrant of inspired prediction (Acts 2:17 KJV), of primitive practice, "And the same man had four daughters, virgins, which did prophesy" (Acts 21:9 KJV), and of apostolic provision, "But every woman that prayeth or prophesieth with her head uncovered dishonoureth her head: for that is even all one as if she were shaven" (1 Cor. 11:5 KJV).

Another interesting review of these verses is ably set forth by Judy L. Brown in her work, Women Ministers According to Scripture. She writes that:

> The silencing of the woman in 1 Corinthians 14:34-35 is conditional and specifically temporary as is that of the glossolalist, for whom silence is preferable to speaking in tongues in the absence of an interpreter (14:28). For the prophet silence is preferable to two prophets fighting for the floor (14:30). The author concludes that the silence that is stipulated in verse 34 is explained or qualified in verse 35, and because this explanation is found within the text itself, it takes precedence over any and all speculative meanings that anyone proposes. He is not imposing an absolute,

universal silence upon half of God's kingdom nor is he barring them from engaging in ministry; he is simply correcting a specific disruptive situation that is evidently present and problematic in the church."[31]

End of Chapter Questions

Chapter V

1. What is the main focus of 1 Corinthians 11:2-16?

2. What was Paul's main concern as expressed in 1 Corinthians 11:2?

3. Define the Greek word *kephale* as used by Paul in 1 Corinthians 11:3.

4. 1 Corinthians 14:34 refers to what?

5. 1 Corinthians 11:5 attests to the fact that women did what?

CHAPTER VI - APOSTLES & PROPHETS

What, exactly, is an Apostle? The Greek word αποστολος, apostolos, simply means messenger or a commissioner of Christ. Apostles are called and separated unto the Gospel (Rom. 1:1), through the will of God (1 Cor. 1:1). Their work is attended to by patience, signs, wonders, and mighty deeds (2 Cor. 12:12). "If I be not an apostle unto others, yet doubtless I am to you: for the seal of mine apostleship are ye in the Lord" (1 Cor. 9:2 KJV), appears to suggest that an Apostle is one who brings the Gospel to a people for the first time and then, perhaps, stays and disciples them until a church is planted. 1 Timothy 1:1 also implies that an Apostle then watches over and instructs the pastor of a local church started as a result of the apostolic ministry.

As Phoebe is mentioned as a minister, or deacon, and is mentioned together with male deacons (Rom. 16:1-16), so, too, it must be noted that a woman is listed among the apostles. Junia was an apostle and fellow prisoner with Paul. Origen of Alexandria is recorded as saying that the name is a variation of the name Julia. This is borne out by Thayer's Greek

Lexicon.[32] The early Greek father, St. John Chrysostom, who was not especially fond of women and generally had negative things to say about them, still spoke positively with regard to Junia. He not only considered Junia to be a female name but penned these words: "Oh, how great is the devotion of this woman, that she should be counted worthy of the appellation of an apostle." This great scholar, in spite of his normal negativity toward women could see the biblical record clearly and had to concede that Junia was, indeed, an Apostle. These aforementioned early scholars were joined by others as listed by Leonard Swidler. He cited Jerome (340-419), Hatto of Verscelli (924-961), Theophylack (1050-1108), and Peter Abelard (1079-1142). Dr. Swidler observed that no one had taken the name to be male until Aegidus of Rome (1245-1316) proffered the idea.[33] That the shadow of male prejudice toward women was cast upon the Old Testament as well as the New Testament can be seen in the Common Version rendering in Psalm 68:11, "The Lord gave the word: great was the company of those that published it," while the Amplified Bible [AMP], The Revised Version [RV], New American Standard [NASB], and the Living Bible [LIV] also concur with the Amplified and use the word "women." The Hebrew צבאה, tseb-aw-aw', is a feminine word that can mean "female host," thus we read the Psalm as: "The Lord gives the word [of power]; the women who bear and publish [the news] are a great host." The Young's Literal Translation [YLT] uses the phrase, "The female proclaimers are a numerous host."

There are, of course, those who argue that women cannot be apostles. Dan Doriani voices his opinion along with many others by saying, "Of all the spiritual gifts in the New Testament, women are able to exercise all of them but that of an apostle."[34] What basis is there for such a statement other than traditional bias on the part of men?

If one woman in the New Testament record can be an Apostle, then what hinders any other woman from following the call of God to the same office? As we mentioned in page ten, the letter of 2 John is clearly written to a woman who is an "elect lady" and an Apostle.

It would also seem that Sister Aimee Semple McPherson was an Apostle. After all, she did found a denomination that is spreading the glorious Gospel even to this day. "In 1927 Mrs. McPherson founded the

International Church of the Foursquare Gospel."[35] She not only founded the denomination but was the final authority on Bible doctrine within it's ranks. This is clearly the work of an Apostle.

If there is any question as to the success of her ministry, her capability, intelligence, or her ability to express sound doctrine, one should read the books she authored as well as her biography.[36]

Now, let's look at the women of the Bible who filled the office of Prophet. It is quite possible that there are more than one might think. Scripture records many women who stood in the ministry office of the Prophet. Here we will consider the ministry of these powerfully anointed women of the Bible and see how God used them in relation to men.

Firstly, I would like to consider Miriam. This amazing woman, along with her brothers, Moses and Aaron, led the children of Israel out of Egypt and across the Red Sea. Micah 6:4 (KJV) shows that the Lord used Miriam as a leader of the people: "For I brought thee up out of the land of Egypt, and redeemed thee out of the house of servants; and I sent before thee Moses, Aaron, and Miriam." She was also referred to in Exodus 15:20 as a prophetess [nebiy'ah], "And Miriam the prophetess, the sister of Aaron, took a timbrel in her hand; and all the women went out after her with timbrels and with dances." The Gesenius' Hebrew Lexicon translates נביאה, nebiy'ah, as a prophetess or (generical) inspired woman; by implication a poetess:- prophetess.[37] She was a prophetess, and a prophetic minstrel but first of all a leader; a leader of women, yes, but also a leader of all of the people along with her brothers.

She was alongside her brothers, Moses and Aaron, as the three together led God's people out of Egypt. Her influence among them was great until she took it upon herself to criticize Moses' marriage to a black Cushite [Ethiopian] woman: "And Miriam and Aaron spake against Moses because of the Ethiopian woman whom he had married: for he had married an Ethiopian woman" (Num. 12:1 KJV). Whether Miriam and Aaron had a problem with her skin color or nationality is of no real importance. Either way, this kind of partiality is a sure path to obscurity for both women and men. That she bore the weight of the punishment for this prejudice was only due to the fact that Aaron wore the garments of a Priest at the time. That God would deal with him later can be seen in Numbers 20:28 (KJV), "And Moses stripped Aaron of his garments, and put them upon Eleazar his son; and Aaron died there in the top of the mount: and Moses and Eleazar came down from the mount."

Then, there is the woman Deborah who not only stood in the office of Prophet but also was the Judge all of Israel. That she was powerful, influential, and courageous is evidenced by the written record that she led Barak, no insignificant man himself, into battle. This man was not weak nor was he afraid of battle or of making decisions. This is readily seen by his ability to hand pick 10,000 soldiers of Zebulun and Naphtali and have them willingly follow him into battle. "And Barak called Zebulun and Naphtali to Kedesh; and he went up with ten thousand men at his feet: and Deborah went up with him" (Judg. 4:10 KJV). It takes a special caliber of man to stand with a woman called of God. He can not be insecure about his masculinity, who he is in God, nor can he be tyrannical in his nature. He must be a man's man who is not threatened by either a strong man or woman who is gifted and/or talented. For our intent and purpose, he must be sure of who he is in Christ and secure in the love of God.

Some men might dare to think that Deborah was not feminine, and certainly not beautiful or lady-like.

There are bound to be those who would consider that she must have been uncomfortably manly, but we see in Judges 4:4 that she was the wife of Lapidoth, whose name indicates that he was quite possibly a prophet himself: "And Deborah, a prophetess, the wife of Lapidoth, she judged Israel at that time." Her husband's name means to shine; a flambeau, lamp or flame :- (fire-) brand, (burning) lamp, lightning, torch.[38] The implication is that he was one who was illumined with prophetic gifting. The prophetic import of the names of Biblical characters is often overlooked.

Great men and women do not follow those they do not respect. Deborah had risen to the most influential position in Israel. It has been noted that "men in her culture did not readily follow women, and few women were allowed to achieve leadership positions."[39] Those who argue against women in ministry and who do not understand how a family can run properly without the husband lording over his wife, rally behind the thinking of a man like Kevin J. Conner who argues for the subordination of women based upon the creative order.[40] Kelly Varner responds, "They say that the woman was created after the man, and is therefore secondary to him. With that same logic, we observe that animals and dirt were created before Adam, yet are not superior to him! . . . Eve completed Adam; she was derived but not inferior. She was not created to serve Adam, but to serve with Adam. As a woman works and rules, she does not lose her femininity but rather regains it."[41] To be a strong woman with leadership ability does not take away from her ability to relate to her husband, nor does it hinder her relationship with other men. Mr. Conner sees the woman as out from under headship as she leads her helpless husband to eat the forbidden fruit and states, "The woman, not the man, was the first to sin, the first and original sinner!"[42] The simple truth is that Satan was the first to sin, and both Adam and Eve willfully bought into his lie and realized death as it's consequence. He interprets the fall as the result of a reversal of the role of husband and wife and fails to see the joint participation in the sinful act. To me, this is myopic.

In an attempt to justify his understanding of Christ, he makes a weak plea emphasizing that other religions suppress women much more than Christianity and that, "Women . . . can minister in many realms except where it involves taking authority over men. Women can minister in the gifts of God as given to her subject to oversight and male headship."[43] This sets forth the dogma that every woman is subject and subservient to not only her husband but to every man. Such a conclusion is ludicrous. Every woman cannot possibly be subject to every man. Imagine the confusion and chaos that would result if your next door neighbor could rule over your wife with the same authority that you, as her husband, hold. Then Mr. Conner, almost apologetically, reaches the conclusion that women can do almost anything men can do "as long as they are under headship."[44]

I like what B. T. Roberts says in his book, Ordaining Women,:

> Prophets and prophetesses rank next to the Apostles. "And God hath set some in the church, first apostles, secondarily prophets" (1 Cor. 12:28 KJV). See also Ephesians 4:11, 12. This last passage declares that God gives them "for the work of the ministry, for the edifying of the body of Christ;" that is for the sanctification of believers and the conversion of sinners. They are also called of God and inspired by His Spirit to preach the Gospel.[45]
>
> Earlier in his text he said, "God only can make

apostles. But if He sends a woman out to do the work of an apostle, and she does it faithfully, why should we hesitate to give the Scriptural name to the office, to fill which she is called and qualified of God?"[46] It is evident that Mr. Roberts is whole-heartedly endorsing women in whatever office God deems fit for them to fill. Be it Apostle, Prophet, Evangelist, Pastor or Teacher, the qualifier is not the gender, but the call.

Now, let's look at another powerful woman who held the office of a prophet. Her name was Huldah, and she was the wife of the keeper of the wardrobe, who lived in Jerusalem's college. The High Priest, scribes, princes, as well as the servant of the King, went to receive of the prophetic ministry of this woman of high estate. The God given words of her mouth shook and shaped the future of the Nation, it's King, leaders and people. "So Hilkiah the priest, and Ahikam, and Achbor, and Shaphan, and Asahiah, went unto Huldah the prophetess, the wife of Shallum the son of Tikvah, the son of Harhas, keeper of the wardrobe; (now she dwelt in Jerusalem in the college;) and they communed with her" (2 Kings 22:14 KJV). Here we find another married woman, an educated woman held in high esteem, clothed upon by the Spirit of the Living God who was sought out by leaders of the nation to discuss the affairs of state, matters of religious significance and to inquire of and receive her counsel as a spokeswoman for God. This flies in the face of the cultural norm and certainly shows that the anointing is respected in whatever vessel upon which it is found to rest.

Q. M. Adams says of her, "Hulda was the right person to consult in this national emergency. She was, apparently, preferred to Jeremiah and Zephaniah, who were both alive at the time and living in Jerusalem."[47] He also makes note of the fact that not all prophets and prophetesses were speaking for God:

> As there were righteous prophets and righteous prophetesses, so there were evil prophets and evil prophetesses.

> Nehemiah denounced Tobiah and Sanballat, with the prophetess Noadiah, and the rest of the prophets who tried to frighten him. (Nehemiah 6:14)

There was also the unnamed prophetess that Isaiah asked "to call her son Maher-shalal-hash-baz, which meant, 'Hasten the spoil, rush on the prey'."[48]

We may also consider the mother of Lemuel the king, who taught him with prophetic insight: "The words of king Lemuel, the prophecy that his mother taught him" (Prov. 31:1 KJV). Although not a great deal is said of her we can glean her prophetic insights, as related to her son, as we read the pages of Proverbs 31. Who can argue with the wisdom expressed in these powerful passages? Should men discount what she has to teach in the sacred writ because the teaching comes from a woman, or should we be able to consider that what she has to say is valid and to be embraced as helpful instruction?

What about Elisabeth, the Cousin of Mary, the mother of our Lord? Although she is not called a prophetess, she certainly did prophesy as she called the babe in Mary's womb, my Lord:

> And it came to pass, that, when Elisabeth heard the salutation of Mary, the babe leaped in her womb; and Elisabeth was filled with the Holy Ghost: And she spake out with a loud voice, and said, Blessed *art* thou among women, and blessed *is* the fruit of thy womb. And whence *is* this to me, that the mother of my Lord should come to me. Luke 1:41- 43 (KJV)

The Holy Spirit had no qualms about anointing her and giving her words of prophetic insight.

Certainly not the least in this list of women, let us consider Mary, a woman well known around the world, the mother of Jesus. This wonderfully blessed woman of faith is also seen moving in the prophetic. As she is moved upon by the Holy Spirit, she voices one of the most powerful prophetic decrees recorded in Scripture, what is known as "The Magnificat." Here she calls her yet unborn son "God my Savior" and decrees the manifold grace of God to His own:

And Mary said, My soul doth magnify the Lord, And my spirit hath rejoiced in God my Savior. For he hath regarded the low estate of his handmaiden: for, behold, from henceforth all generations shall call me blessed. For he that is mighty hath done to me great things; and holy *is* his name. And his mercy *is* on them that fear him from generation to generation. He hath shewed strength with his arm; he hath scattered the proud in the imagination of their hearts. He hath put down the mighty from *their* seats, and exalted them of low degree. He hath filled the hungry with good things; and the rich he hath sent empty away. He hath holpen his servant Israel, in remembrance of *his* mercy; As he spake to our fathers, to Abraham, and to his seed for ever. Luke 1:46-55 (KJV)

Let us not forget the woman who was privileged to be serving in the temple at Jerusalem when Mary and Joseph brought the Christ child to be circumcised. This precious, powerful, and faithful woman of God knew before hand that the Christ of God was coming to the Temple and had been watching and waiting with fasting and prayer for forty-four years. As Simeon came by the Spirit to see Israel's Messiah, so also Anna the prophetess came at that same instant:

> And there was one Anna, a prophetess, the daughter of Phanuel, of the tribe of Aser: she was of a great age, and had lived with an husband seven years from her virginity; And she was a widow of about fourscore and four years, which departed not from the temple, but served God with fastings and prayers night and day. And she coming in that instant gave thanks likewise unto the Lord, and spake of him to all them that looked for redemption in Jerusalem. Luke 2:36-38 (KJV)

This faithful, God fearing woman was rewarded for her consistent heart felt service in the temple with a visit from the King of kings, and the Lord of lords. She was the first recorded witness of the Redeemer of Israel and the world as she testified of Him "to all them that looked for redemption in Jerusalem."

Let us consider too, the four unnamed virgins who were the daughters of Philip the evangelist. They were not necessarily prophets but were notable in that they were recognized as flowing in the prophetic. "And the same man had four daughters, virgins, which did prophesy" (Acts 21:9 KJV).

The preceding examples of women who God chose to speak through should give us ample basis for accepting the prophetic gifting in women of today. The following verses of Scripture gleaned from the New Testament also provide solid evidence for accepting prophetic utterance without regard to the gender of the vessel God chooses to use. "Despise not prophesyings" (1 Thess. 5:20 KJV). "Follow after charity, and desire spiritual *gifts,* but rather that ye may prophesy" (1 Cor. 14:1 KJV). "Wherefore, brethren, covet to prophesy, and forbid not to speak with tongues" (1 Cor. 14:39 KJV).

The prophetic should never be disdained nor despised, for the testimony of Jesus is the Spirit of prophecy. "And I fell at his feet to worship him. And he said unto me, See thou do it not: I am thy fellow servant, and of thy brethren that have the testimony of Jesus: worship God: for the testimony of Jesus is the spirit of prophecy" (Rev. 19:10 KJV). This ministry of the prophetic is set in the church so that all may learn and be comforted. The exercise of simple prophecy is a ministry by which all are encouraged to engage in one by one.

As it is written, "For ye may all prophesy one by one, that all may learn, and all may be comforted. And the spirits of the prophets are subject to the prophets" (1 Cor. 14:31-32 KJV). "All" is inclusive of both men and women as is the reference to the spirits of the prophets.

We learn in 1 Chronicles 16:22 that both male and female prophets are watched over and protected by Almighty God and that we are to honor them and give place for their ministry. To do them dishonor and give no place for the expression of their gifting and calling can bring disastrous results as God Himself positions Himself to protect His chosen ones, "Saying, Touch not mine anointed, and do my prophets no harm" [also Psalm 105:15]. Jesus, Himself, said that there is a reward for those who are receptive to the prophet and his or her ministry. "He that receiveth a prophet in the name of a prophet shall receive a prophet's reward" (Matt. 10:41 KJV).

The prophetic ministry is given to guide, direct, admonish, correct, and otherwise give voice to the plan and purpose of God. It is not a destructive ministry but one of edification that brings what is necessary to bring about complete redemption. Here we can refer to Amos 3:7 where we read, "Surely the Lord GOD will do nothing, but he revealeth his secret unto his servants the prophets" (KJV).

Prophets move within the proportion of faith that they have, as is with all gifts and graces of the Spirit. Some move very accurately, powerfully, and authoritatively while others are less sure and developed in their office or gift. No one has absolute clarity in bringing forth the word of God, "For we know in part, and we prophesy in part" (1 Cor. 13:9 KJV). "Having then gifts differing according to the grace that is given to us, whether prophecy, let us prophesy according to the proportion of faith" (Rom. 12:6 KJV).

God sets offices in the church without regard to age, nationality, class, gender, or color. "There is neither Jew nor Greek, there is neither bond nor free, there is neither male nor female: for ye are all one in Christ Jesus" (Gal. 3:28 KJV). This verse and its companion bring to light the simple truth that the race, class nor gender of those commissioned by God has nothing to do with their ability to fulfill their call. "For in Christ Jesus neither circumcision availeth anything, nor uncircumcision, but a new creature" (Gal. 6:15 KJV). The "Lord seeth not as man seeth; for man looketh on the outward appearance, but the Lord looketh on the heart" (1 Sam. 16:7 KJV). Remember, it is God alone that chooses and then gives gifts to men. "And he gave some, apostles; and some, prophets; and some, evangelists; and some, pastors and teachers" (Eph. 4:11 KJV).

Our heavenly Father would not tell all of his children to desire something that He would only give to some. He is not a respecter of persons. When we read of the "promise of the Father" mentioned in Luke 24:49, and again in Acts 1:4, being poured out in the upper room on the day of Pentecost in, they all [men, women and children] were filled with the Spirit and spoke with other tongues. Yes, men, women and children were in the upper room. Let's read Acts 1:13-14 (KJV):

And when they were come in, they went up into an upper room, where abode both Peter, and James, and John, and Andrew, Philip, and Thomas, Bartholomew, and Matthew, James the son of Alphaeus, and Simon Zelotes, and Judas the brother of James. These all continued with one accord in prayer and supplication, with the women, and Mary the mother of Jesus, and with his brethren.

This event, as recorded in the second chapter of the book of Acts, was the evidence that they received the Baptism in the Holy Spirit and would now flow in the gifts of the Spirit:

But the manifestation of the Spirit is given to every man to profit withal. For to one is given by the Spirit the word of wisdom; to another the word of knowledge by the same Spirit; To another faith by the same Spirit; to another the gifts of healing by the same Spirit; To another the working of miracles; to another prophecy; to another discerning of spirits; to another *divers* kinds of tongues; to another the interpretation of tongues: But all these worketh that one and the selfsame Spirit, dividing to every man severally as he will. For as the body is one, and hath many members, and all the members of that one body, being many, are one body: so also *is* Christ. For by one Spirit are we all baptized into one body, whether *we be* Jews or Gentiles, whether *we be* bond or free; . . . [male or female]. 1 Corinthians 12:7-13 (KJV).[49]

The word man: is the Greek word εκαστος, "hekastos, hek'-as-tos; as if a superlative of hekas (afar); each or every:- any, both, each (one), every (man, one, woman), particularly."[50] As we can see, more often than not, the word man is denoting male and female. We also learn here that the Holy Spirit gives what and to whom He wills.

End of Chapter Questions
Chapter VI

1. Junia was listed as an apostle and fellow prisoner with Paul. What early scholars verified that "Junia" was a female name?

2. Amee Semple McPherson was the founding apostle of what denomination?

3. Who led the children of God out of Egypt along with Moses and Aaron?

4. List the women who were listed as prophetesses in this chapter.

5. What three verses in the New Testament provide solid evidence for accepting prophetic utterance with out regard to the gender of the vessel God chooses to use?

6. Define the Greek word, εκαστος, *hekastos*.

CHAPTER VII – PREJUDICE

As we continue to consider this still very much alive topic of the rightful place of men and women in ministry consider with me, if you will, the word prejudice. According to the <u>Doubleday Dictionary</u>, the word prejudice finds it root in the original Latin <u>praejudicium</u>, from <u>prae</u> "in advance" plus <u>judicium</u> "judgement." This word means, "1. A judgment or opinion formed without due examination of facts, etc. 2. An unreasonable judgment held despite facts to the contrary. 3. Fear of and hatred for other races, religions, etc.,"[51] or, a preconceived opinion that is not based on reason or experience and unjust behavior formed on such a basis. Prejudice of any kind is completely unacceptable in light of Scripture. Jesus shattered every prejudice that was prevalent in His day. He met the prevailing prejudices of gender, race and national origin at the well in Samaria, as he spoke with the woman at the well in John 4:4-27. During that particular period of time, a righteous Jew would never go to Samaria, let alone speak with a Samaritan, especially a female Samaritan. Jesus not only went to a nationality considered to be unclean outcasts but was seeking to meet and speak with them. He shattered the long held national prejudices that ruled in His day and went further by speaking to a woman of that culture about spiritual things. This act is understood to be a thought out purposeful blow at the gender bias of Jewish tradition. In books like <u>Life in The Father's House</u>, by Mack A. Wayne and David Swavely, we are told that women were "esteemed and lauded in ancient Israel." Actually, the opposite was true. This can be readily grasped as one reads the scholarly work of David Joel Hamilton on pages 101 through 109 in the recently released book <u>Why Not Women?</u>.[52] In his chapter on "Distorting the Image," Mr. Hamilton states that the Jew, Philo of Alexandria, mixed the writings of Aristotle and Moses. He writes, "Jews built 'walls' to protect their religious beliefs." Rabbinical oral traditions were gathered in the Mishnah. "Soon those walls weren't enough, so walls were built around walls, outer defenses to protect inner defenses." The thinking behind the oral traditions was that the Mishna and Talmud could build "ramparts of ritual" that would preserve Jewish faith from the Gentiles more than that of an army. He went on to say:

The rabbis didn't always agree with one

another in either the Mishnah or the opinions that made up the Talmud. Their writings were filled with heated arguments that continued for generations. Some of these debates were about women. At times, the arguments were based upon the account in Genesis, and the value of women was upheld. More often, though, the rabbis strayed from the values shown in Genesis. They heaped scorn upon Eve, claiming that the serpent had sex with her, and this had "infused her with lust." Although Genesis showed the essential unity between men and women, the rabbis preferred to point out the differences.[53]

He also believed that history shows that mankind has always been prone to read their own cultural values into Scripture rather than looking at God's Word and forming cultural values from it. The rabbis seemed to have done the former, saying, "Compared with Adam, Eve was like a monkey to a human being."[54] Eventually their belief in male superiority had so distorted their teaching that their words were filled with poison. Ideas like, "A man must be saved alive sooner than a woman, and his lost property must be restored sooner than hers," "Ten <u>kabs</u> of gossip descended to the world: nine were taken by women," and "Woe to him who has female children! A daughter is like a trap for her father . . .," were stated as gospel truth.[55] It went so far that there were a group of Pharisees who were called the "Bleeding Pharisees" because they believed that even the little finger of a woman was sexual, and so would close their eyes while passing a woman and then run into things to their own hurt.[56] These, and more, were the teachings that formed the religious mind set of the day in which Jesus lived.

The Samaritan people were a people of mixed race and so we are also viewing the Lord's utter disdain for racial divisions. This momentous event and the conclusions regarding the prejudices dealt with there are ably brought to light in the preface of Kelly Varner's book, <u>The Three Prejudices</u> where the author notes that:

> Prejudice is anything that separates us from God and each other. Prejudice is learned behavior. Men have discovered how to build all kinds of walls. Prejudice is hate, and it is based upon the spirit of fear. Its underlying essence is insecurity–the fear of rejection, of not being

accepted.

Prejudice is "pre-judgment," an opinion formed before the facts are known. It is unreasonable bias. Prejudice is bigotry, discrimination, intolerance, narrow-mindedness, opinion, partiality. Prejudice is poison. Prejudice is the innate, corrupted character of the old Adamic nature that causes men to choose whom they love. Prejudice has to do with character, the heart condition of the inner man. Prejudice is ingrained in us. It is the thing that knots up in our gut and really upsets us when we hear the truth. Prejudice pushes our buttons and rings our bell. Prejudice can never be surmounted by human means. The only real, lasting cure for this unholy spirit is the love of God. The single antidote for this spirit of anti-christ is the supernatural, dynamic, life-changing power of the Holy Spirit. The only remedy for this universal human need is the personal and collective experience of the love of God–being forgiven, accepted in the Beloved, safe and secure in Christ.[57]

This same sentiment is voiced by Dr. Fuchia

Pickett as she declares, "There was nothing to which Jesus laid the ax more violently than the traditions of men."[58] The traditions of men become interwoven with religious belief and become the destructive dogma that Jesus strove against. He was ever calling the religious of His day to return to that which was given by God and to live in the light of its truth:

> Ye are the salt of the earth: but if the salt have lost his savour, wherewith shall it be salted? it is thenceforth good for nothing, but to be cast out, and to be trodden under foot of men. Ye are the light of the world. A city that is set on an hill cannot be hid. Neither do men light a candle, and put it under a bushel, but on a candlestick; and it giveth light unto all that are in the house. Let your light so shine before men, that they may see your good works, and glorify your Father which is in heaven.

> Think not that I am come to destroy the law, or the prophets: I am not come to destroy, but to fulfil. For verily I say unto you, Till heaven and earth pass, one jot or one tittle shall in no wise pass from the law, till all be fulfilled.

> Whosoever therefore shall break one of

these least commandments, and shall teach men so, he shall be called the least in the kingdom of heaven: but whosoever shall do and teach them, the same shall be called great in the kingdom of heaven. Matthew 5:13-19 (KJV)

The Gospel of Jesus Christ, in the hearts of learned and spiritual men, has been the only true liberator of women in the history of mankind. Women were reduced in estimation to no more than property, chattel, servants, and slaves in almost every culture, with the possible exception of pagan goddess-worshipers. Today, this traditional prejudice is held by the adherents to Islam, Judaism, Mormonism, and many religious groups in the world. Jesus came and decreed that there were no distinctions and that men and women were to be treated as equals. One of the great hallmarks of Christianity is that it liberates women bound by pagan religious tradition in the societies where it finds fertile ground. It is only in the manipulating of Scripture out of context that some, so called, Christian groups hold women in bondages similar to those found in pagan culture. This must cause Satan to rejoice at his ability to cloud the clear intent of the liberating Word of God in the minds of religious men, keeping them from realizing the great benefit that can be realized by releasing women into the ministry.

It would seem that the unwillingness or hesitancy to allow women a full place at the Lord's Table is, in some cases, tied to man's inability to subdue his own passions. Many men are either unwilling or unable to look upon a woman without stirring lustful thoughts. This is not the modestly dressed woman's problem, but the man's. In this day of too much television, too many movies, and ready access to internet pornography, the problem is only exacerbated. One might think that this is a frivolous observation, but when considered in the light of the thinking of past traditions and the fact that 65 percent of the pastors in America are hooked on internet pornography, it is something to consider.[59]

For too long the great strength of our sisters in Christ have been relegated to those areas where they do not threaten the male dominated perceptions of propriety. Stan Guthrie, in his article A Woman's Place In Missions, noted that "This situation is due in part to a theological view called complementarianism. It holds that while men and women are equal in the sight of God in terms of dignity and value, they have different roles."[60] He also stated that others argue, among whom I align myself, "that gender distinctions were obliterated at the cross," and cites Galatians 3:28 as proof, "There is neither Jew nor Greek, there is neither bond nor free, there is neither male nor female: for ye are all one in Christ Jesus" (Gal. 3:28 KJV). Herbert Lockyer and many other early scholars and authors held to the complementarianistic view. We read Mr Lockyer saying, "Priority of creation gave Adam headship but not superiority" and then, as though he might have had second thoughts says on the same page, "Both man and woman were endowed for equality and for mutual interdependence."[61] If you think this sounds a little bit schizophrenic, I would have to agree. Equal does not necessarily mean same or like copy of. Even differences in calling are equal in importance and equally dependent upon a daily anointing.

The priority in creation argument loses it's logic when one considers that animals, birds and fish were all created prior to man. This obviously does not place humanity in a subservient or subject position with relation to the animals. After all, Adam gave them their character by naming them. Using Mr. Lockyer's logic would place any one, or all, of them in a headship, "but not superiority," position. Hardly an edifying thought, now is it?

Mr. Guthrie goes on to note that there have been "many great works led by gifted women" and the question is asked "whether it is God's will that these ministries be terminated." Before you, or I, answer too quickly it would be good to note that the Four Square Gospel denomination founded by Aimee Semple MacPherson would need to be disbanded.

George Verwer was quoted in the same publication, "Virtually every mission agency operating around the globe is desperate for more workers. This raises the question: 'Why are there so few workers available for such an enormous task?'."[62] Perhaps it is, as Mr. Guthrie wrote,

> Women have always been at the heart of the missionary enterprise. One need only mention names such as Rosalind Goforth, Mary Slessor, Rachel Saint, and Betty Stam to understand the truth of such a statement. In terms of decision-making, however, missions has been a male domain. Few mission boards have a female CEO, even though women missionaries are more numerous than males, making up two-

thirds of the missionary force.[63]

It would appear that men want to govern in areas where they are unwilling to serve and rule where they have not toiled. This is not Christian in its attitude or practice. Scriptures like Luke 10:7, which says, "the labourer is worthy of his hire," and 1 Timothy 5:18 which adds, "The labourer is worthy of his reward," teach us that it is the one who does the work that is worthy of their hire and that the laborer is the one worthy of reward. I believe it would be of benefit to here define the word "reward:" μισθος, misthos, which carries the idea of: "dues paid for work, wages, hire, the fruit naturally resulting from toils and endeavours, of the rewards which God bestows, or will bestow, upon good deeds and endeavours."[64]

Dan Doriani, Professor of New Testament and Dean of Faculty at Covenant Theological Seminary in St. Louis, Missouri, and others like him, state that women can lead in a crisis, but at the same time "must work to end the crisis by seeking a male leader, rather than functioning indefinitely on her own."[65] This implies that a crisis can be ended by bringing in a male leader. Female leadership is implied in Acts 18:18, 26 as well as in Romans 16:1-3, where Phebe is named as

-111-

a "minister," or "deacon," διακονος, diakonos, and Aquila's wife was named before he was. This would imply that she was the leader in their teaching ministry.

And Paul after this tarried there yet a good while, and then took his leave of the brethren, and sailed thence into Syria, and with him Priscilla and Aquila; having shorn his head in Cenchrea: for he had a vow. Acts 18:18 (KJV)

And he began to speak boldly in the synagogue: whom when Aquila and Priscilla had heard, they took him unto them, and expounded unto him the way of God more perfectly. Acts 18:26 (KJV)

I commend unto you Phebe our sister, which is a servant of the church which is at Cenchrea: That ye receive her in the Lord, as becometh saints, and that ye assist her in whatsoever business she hath need of you: for she hath been a succourer of many, and of myself also. Greet Priscilla and Aquila my helpers in Christ Jesus: Romans 16:1-3 (KJV)

Doctor Doriani also joins the all male choir singing the very much over-worked "first created" argument, therefore concluding that, "male leadership is

God's original plan. It is not due to the Fall and the curse."[66] He also holds the view that women should never hold public positions in the church or elsewhere, for that matter. He maintains that women should lead only alongside men. He says, "women teach and lead in the covenant family, but they do not hold a permanent public teaching office." Mr. Doriani then goes on to say, "If our Lord can submit to the Father without losing any dignity or value, then women can submit to male leaders while they have equal knowledge, holiness, and worth."[67] We could also consider that the opposite would then be true also. A man could submit to a woman as would be the case as stated in 2 John 1:10. We read where Paul was instructing Junia the Apostle as to how to deal with men who spread untruths, "If there come any unto you, and bring not this doctrine, receive him not into your house, neither bid him God speed." The obvious submission of, and dependency upon, each member of the Godhead to the other should suffice to set this argument aside.

I will never forget how I felt when I read the testimony of Jackie Pullinger, a young British girl, in her book <u>Chasing the Dragon</u>. She spent her life in Hong Kong investing in the lives of those addicted to opium and built a sizeable work only to be told by her denomination that a man should come take over now that the work was built.[68] It is very difficult for me to find a thread of workable logic in this kind of thinking. Wasn't it Paul, the man that some have accused of being a woman hater, who said, "Yea, so have I strived to preach the gospel, not where Christ was named, lest I should build upon another man's foundation" (Rom. 15:20 KJV). He believed in plowing his own field and not trying to appropriate a field that had been worked by another. He admonished, instructed, and encouraged those who he had won, trained and established as pastors, overseers, etc., and churches that he had planted. Ms. Pullinger plowed, planted, watered, and now should have had the privilege of harvesting the fruit of her labor; not turn it over to a man. It is written, "They that sow in tears shall reap in joy" (Psa. 126:5 KJV).

You may believe that such prejudices are a thing of the past. I would that they were, but, unfortunately, many still hold to old prejudices with an unnatural, almost superhuman, tenacity. My wife and I have long ago worked out our relationship as 'called ones' of God. The two of us pastor Wellspring Church of All

Nations. We don't jostle over who is going to lead, who is going to administrate, who is going to preach. We have learned to seek the face of God and find our answers in Him. She is as capable a minister as any I have ever met. Her integrity is above reproach and that sets her high above many that mount the pulpits of today's churches. In spite of her calling, three earned Doctorates, total support by me, and acceptance by the church, she still is treated as less than in some circles.

We attended a funeral for a dear pastor friend of ours who held her in high regard and treated her as an equal. Our ministerial fellowship was going to honor him and many of the leaders of our region had come to pay their respects. As the various Fellowship members and ministers were moving toward the platform she was told, "You need to go sit in the back with the other women." She politely said, "I'm a minister in this fellowship too," only to have the directive repeated with added severity. When I told those in charge that she was a minister, a member of their organization, and a friend of the deceased, they acted as if I had never said a word and again suggested that she just sit back with the other women where she belonged. I repeated what I said and those in charge finally yielded and allowed her join the other ministers on the platform and we acted as though nothing had happened.

These demeaning incidences should never happen in the body of Christ. We are taught that the proper way to esteem one another is that of, "Submitting yourselves one to another in the fear of God" (Eph. 5:21 KJV). Even after such an uncomfortable situation, we decided to stay with that particular fellowship of ministers because we knew that things were changing and that we could help to bring complete liberty to all of its members. I am very pleased to say that this prejudice, along with others, is rapidly passing away and the Fellowship is now moving in new anointing and power as the membership is learning to follow the Spirit of Liberty and Truth. Liberty is the promise given to all believers, not just the men. This is readily seen in the words, "Now the Lord is that Spirit: and where the Spirit of the Lord is, there is liberty" (2 Cor. 3:17 KJV).

We have also had many occasions where visitors would come to our church services only to get up and leave when they realized that a woman was going to preach. Sadly, they missed one of the most well versed and anointed preachers of this hour and, quite possibly, their healing besides. This makes evident the reality that many pulpits are still preaching a prejudiced gospel concerning women in ministry. This is no wonder considering that the leaders of many of today's seminaries dispense the same philosophy as the aforementioned Dr. Doriani. His Doctorate allows him the ear of many a student as he sets forth his supposedly learned conclusions such as, "we can conclude that women can lead in various ways, but men must be responsible for doctrine and the direction of the church," or "Women may occasionally teach men, as long as they do so under the authority of a male leader. For example, a woman could serve as a guest speaker to a men's Sunday school class, but should not teach it regularly."[69] These conclusions are bereft of scriptural support and simply parrot what his mentor's traditions have passed on. Gender bias, like racism, is taught. It is a generational curse that is easily acquired but very, very difficult to be delivered of.

Many women meet a man, marry, and quickly move into the traditionally accepted help-meet position of backing, undergirding, or completing their husbands. This is both natural and fulfilling in that women have been designed by their Creator to come along side and complete. But then, isn't that what all Christians are called to do?

In today's world a woman may even enter the market place and pursue a career while maintaining their conventional status quo at home. The thing that seems to upset the apple cart, so to speak, is when they become aware of a call into the ministry. Many of the women that I have spoken to over the years tell me that they are quite happy to be a wife to their husbands and a mother to their children. They have no other interest and are completely satisfied in their roles. This is commendable in that they are fulfilling their assignment, their calling, in life. Even when they work outside the home, they still see themselves primarily as wife, mother and help to their husbands. Almost every woman that receives a call of God on her life, however, seems to be forced to run a gauntlet of misunderstanding and abuse even though they have not left off their care for husband or family. Way too many women are living with a hidden desire to serve God in a manner that is unacceptable to the men in their lives. Too many are coerced into being men pleasers rather than God pleasers in a perverted submission to their, so-called, head.

Perhaps women should be given more credit than is normally allowed them. According to a survey conducted by the highly respected Barna Research Group, it was found that women prove to be much more spiritually inclined than men. There may be many men who would contest such findings, yet the facts do speak for themselves.

Females were more likely to say they were absolutely committed to Christianity (10 percentage points higher than men), read the Bible (+ 10 percentage points), attend church (+11 points), pray to God (+13 points), participate in a small group (+ 7 points), and have a quiet time (+14 points). The differences between the two genders were statistically insignificant regarding volunteering at church, attending Sunday school and sharing their faith. Men were much more likely to be unchurched (38% vs. 29%), meaning that they had not attended a church service other than for a special event such as a wedding or funeral at any time in the past six months. Women were also more likely than were men to be born again by a 45% to 36% margin.[70]

This is not just a new phenomena can only be applied to our current culture. In the 1800's, a skeptic of women in ministry was heard, quite surprisingly enough, to say:

> I tell you women are more prudent than men. I tell you, as a rule, women are more truthful than men. I tell you that women are more faithful than men–ten times as faithful as men. I never saw a man pursue his wife into the very ditch and dust of degradation and take her in his arms. I never saw a man stand at the shore where she had been morally wrecked, waiting for the waves to bring back even her corpse to his arms; but I have seen woman do it. I have seen woman with her white arms lift man from the mire of degradation, and hold him to her bosom as though he were an angel.[71]

A casual glance at most any church service or Christian convention will attest to the fact that there are quite a few more women pursuing God than men. This has been the case for as long as there has been a record of the spread of the Gospel message. Although Jesus purposefully gathered men around Him, He was ministered to and attended to by women much of the time.

Wouldn't it follow that if women have this God given propensity toward the things of the Lord, they should be allowed to express their faith? Or are we men so intimidated by women that we cannot allow ourselves to even consider the possibility? Can we put aside preconceived ideas and perceptions, prejudices, and be open enough to research the Scripture with an unbiased heart and mind?

End of Chapter Questions
Chapter VII

1. Define the English word, "prejudice."
2. Can you find any prejudices in your life that might influence your interpretation of the scriptural record?
3. What is the meaning of the theological view called, "complementarianism?"
4. What did you think, or feel, as you read Jackie Pullinger's story?
5. What was your reaction to Barna Research group's findings?

"Covenant" by Patricia Rios

CHAPTER VIII - WOMEN OF INFLUENCE

Many have been the women that have exerted great influence on our nation and others. They have shaped the course of history by their courage, tenacity and faith. Leaders of nations, and the population of whole countries have been given direction by their teaching and guidance. It is quite possible that, in many cases, husbands and sons became influential leaders because of the input and effect of their mothers or wives. It has been said that, "behind every great man is a great woman." This is a saying worth contemplating considering that the woman of Genesis was a help meet [עֵזֶר 'ezer] for the man. This word means, a helper, a succourer [one who assists and supports in times of hardship and distress; one who gives assistance to]. This is a companion perfectly adapted and suited for her spouse.

Although one would be hard pressed to find evidence that France was once a Christian nation, yet it is true. France was known as a Christian nation after a woman exerted her influence on the King and the people. It was through the evangelization of Clotilde, a Burgundian princess, a Christian, who married Clovis, a great warrior, a pagan, and the King of the Franks. She won her husband and won her nation.[72] It is worthy of our attention how much influence a mere wife has to change an entire nation. Both Mac Hammond, pastor of Living Word Christian Center in Minneapolis, Minnesota, and internationally known author, and John Maxwell, well known lecturer and author, state that, "Leadership is influence. Nothing more and nothing less." If this is true, then Clotilde was definitely a leader.

Abraham Lincoln's stepmother, Sarah Bush Lincoln, and his mother, Nancy, both encouraged him to read the Bible and learn all he could. His mother once said, "I would rather my son would be able to read the Bible than to own a farm, if he cannot have but one." Although Lincoln professed Christ relatively late in life, he did indeed read the Bible a great deal and often used it as the foundation of speeches. He once called it "the best gift God has given to man."

Lincoln always turned to his faith during the most difficult times of his life. After seeking the Lord concerning the North's lack of success during the Civil War, the revelation he received caused him to issue the Emancipation Proclamation, freeing the slaves in all territories still at war with the Union. He also called for national repentance, fasting, and prayer. This president had a monumental impact on our country. He attributed his achievements to the person who influenced him most by saying, "All that I am, or hope to be, I owe to my angel mother. I remember my mother's prayers and they have always followed me. They have clung to me all my life."[73] Those who influence are those who, in actuality, lead. "Harriet Tubman came to be called Moses because of her ability to go into the land of captivity and bring so many of her people out of slavery's bondage." In 1857, three hundred slaves followed her to freedom out of the South. They recognized and respected her leadership.[74] This was a woman of great influence, and therefore, a great leader.

George Washington's mother was another one of those wonderful women who, through her influence upon her son, changed the leadership of the nation. "His mother had been a strong source of spiritual life in his early years. On the day he left home to begin a lifetime of serving his country, she said to him: 'Remember that God only is our sure trust. To Him, I commend you.' and then she added, 'My son, neglect not the duty of secret prayer.'"[75] Leaders lead by influencing others to follow their training and example.

The historical record is full of women like:

Antoinette L. Brown (1825-1921), a convert of Charles Finney (who encouraged women to speak in mixed assemblies), who was the first American woman to be ordained a minister. This took place at the Congregational Church of South Butler, New York, on September 15, 1853. At the time of her death, 68 years after her ordination, there were more than 3,000 women ministers in the United States."[76]

The life and ministry of Maria Woodworth-Etter is recorded in her book, A Diary of Signs and Wonders. We read of her:

Maria Woodworth-Etter was a great Pentecostal fore-runner. Born in 1844, she began to minister the gospel in her mid-twenties. By the late 1880s (and before her personal Pentecostal experience), she was preaching to tent crowds of 20,000 or more. She pioneered dozens of churches and licensed other preachers, pastoring in Indianapolis from 1918 until her death in 1924.[77]

One can hardly refute the effect of the preaching

and ministry of Dr. Billy Graham. He has earned the right to be heard in every nation of the world and is esteemed as one of the most trustworthy men of God in modern time. He testifies:

> That Dr. Henrietta Mears influenced his life more than any other woman besides his own wife and his mother. Dr. Mears established the Gospel Light Press and put teachings into print that are being taught all over the world - even in churches where men are teaching who don't believe in women teachers![78]

In India, testimony was given concerning a woman by the name of Pandita Ramabai who "was mightily anointed with the Holy Spirit. This woman had many evangelistic, healing meetings and a mission in Kedgaon, India."[79] She influenced, and therefore led, many men and women to go higher in God.

The great evangelist John Wesley was mightily influenced and encouraged by his mother.[80] The results of that influence can still be seen and heard in the Church today.

There were a "few courageous southern women who risked cruel ostracism to record their testimony - Fanny Kemble, Anne Page, Kate Stone, Mary Chesnut, and the Grimke sisters." These women spoke without ranting or slanting, a simple presentation of the horrendous facts and testimonies of slavery, and let their stories speak for themselves.[81]

There have been several women that have influenced my life and the lives of many others. One of the first ladies that I came into contact with was Katheryn Khulman. This woman's healing crusades swept the nation and the world. I will never forget when she came to Las Vegas, Nevada in 1975. My wife and I had only been born-again a couple of years and went to see why so many people would flock to her meetings. We sat high in the balcony of the Las Vegas Convention Center dome and could only see her as a tiny figure far below. As she began to minister there was a wind that began to blow throughout the building. It was not a natural wind, not the air-conditioning coming on, not an open door, but the wind of the Holy Spirit. There was a powerful conviction of sin and the healing virtue of Christ Jesus was touching people all over the building. People started flooding to the altar to testify of the marvelous works of God. My life was impacted by the reality of the work of the Holy Spirit and, subsequently, by reading many of her books and pamphlets. She had led me into the things of the spirit by word and deed. By her influence she had become the teacher and leader of many because, "influence is leadership. Nothing more and nothing less."[82] Roberts Lairdon records of her:

Kathryn Kuhlman was unique, although she called herself an ordinary person. . . . Many have tried to imitate her voice and her theatrical mannerisms but have failed. Many have tried to translate the anointing that was on her into techniques and methods, but that has not been possible. Those attempting to copy her have had no power, no anointing. . . . Kathryn was a woman of great humility.

She was careful to give God all of the glory for everything that occurred in her life and ministry. She stated consistently that the healings which occurred through her ministry were not her doing but the work of God. People came forward in her meetings to testify of their healings - not to receive healing.[83]

Maryiann Sitton, founder of Shiloh Christian Ministries, Shiloh Retreat, and Shiloh Training Institute is another woman that changed my life and the perceptions I had of women ministers. Her Bible School was an anointed place where several of our church staff ministers were trained. We released them to go to Montana to be schooled at Shiloh and received them back filled with the Holy Ghost and well equipped for the work of the ministry. Her prophetic ministry spoke into the life of my wife and I many times and kept us from making serious mistakes along the way. One phone call to, or from, this wonderful lady would bring great wisdom to almost any situation. She was anointed to lead by example and by the teaching of her words.

Katherine Haubert is a wonderful woman of God and a dear friend of mine. After attending Shiloh Training Institute, she went to Fuller Theological Seminary in Pasadena, California and earned her Doctorate. She has authored a book on women in ministry and served as an Associate Pastor for the Vineyard Fellowship of Orange Country for years.[84] Now she has drawn together a church planting team and has been sent out by her denomination to plant a work in Wisconsin. She is a capable and well trained minister of the Gospel and a member of the Wellspring Ministerial Fellowship. Her heart to serve the Lord is evidenced in all that she does.

Margaret Van Camp is another powerful woman who is Pastor of Church of All Nations in Hayward, California. She is well respected by the international community and has influenced the lives of countless men and women for Christ.

Billye Brim, Joyce Meyer, Gloria Copeland, Marylin Hickey, June Evans, Rebeca Hood, and many other anointed and powerful women of God are impacting the world for the cause of Christ as they influence the leaders of nations. They come flowing in the anointing for this hour and work with men and women alike. The church would be greatly weakened without their gifts, talents, and energies lending their strength as they lead in the Body of Christ.

In the next Chapter we will look at the Biblical and historical record of some of the many women of faith and reconsider any anti-female attitudes, concepts and positions, that may be keeping you from releasing this large and vibrant segment of the Body of Christ. Allow yourself to consider the creativity and fortitude with which these women dealt with the difficult situations in their lives. Consider, too, the way Jesus treated, and responded to, women during His time on earth. They were always attending him and were given great responsibility in carrying out the work of the early church. Their personal ministry to Him showed far more holy passion and personal sacrifice than did that of many of His male companions.

"Forgiven" by Patricia Rios

End of Chapter Questions
Chapter VIII

1. The Hebrew word, עֵזֶר, *'ezer*, means.

2. What French woman won her husband to Christ and changed the nation?

3. Who was the first American woman to be ordained?

4. What well known men were influenced by the women in their lives?

5. What woman has, or women have, influenced your spiritual life? In what way?

CHAPTER IX - NOTABLE WOMEN IN SCRIPTURE

There are several women mentioned in the Bible that are not considered to be ministers or leaders of their people and yet it might be appropriate to mention the important roles that these women of faith played in the plan of God. It will be seen that their integrity, resourcefulness, tact, wisdom, and courage neither made them less womanly nor did it cause those of them who were married to act unbecomingly toward their husbands. Each of these are women of significance in the Scriptures and portray qualities that do make for good leaders. Much can be learned as we consider the events of their lives and how they handled them.

Jael was a remarkable woman and was instrumental in the crushing of the captain of Jabin's army as she, in fulfillment of the prophetic utterance of Deborah, drove a tent peg through Sisera's head. Her quick thinking and willingness to act in a difficult situation caused her to be recorded in the Book of Books. Although this woman was not noted as a leader, the ability to evaluate a situation and act accordingly is a necessary leadership quality. While Herbert Lockyer sees her as a reprehensible murderer, I will align myself with the Bible's silence on such accusation and speak of her willingness to join in vanquishing the enemies of her people according to prophetic decree of Deborah.[85]

> And she said, I will surely go with thee: notwithstanding the journey that thou takest shall not be for thine honour; for the LORD shall sell Sisera into the hand of a woman. And Deborah arose, and went with Barak to Kedesh. Judges 4:9 (KJV)

Then, there was the Shunammite woman who was called "great." Why? Though the Scriptural record does not reveal exactly what makes her great in her society, we can see that she was wise enough to encourage her husband to make provision for the prophet of God. The subsequent blessing upon their house was directly tied to her decision. We know from the New Testament record in Matthew 10:41 (KJV) that one of the principles of God is that "He that receiveth a prophet in the name of a prophet shall receive a prophet's reward." She is also recorded as being a woman of great faith in that when her son died she said, "It is well," knowing that God was well able to raise her son from the dead:

And it fell on a day, that Elisha passed to Shunem, where was a great woman; and she constrained him to eat bread. And so it was, that as oft as he passed by, he turned in thither to eat bread. And she said unto her husband, Behold now, I perceive that this is an holy man of God, which passeth by us continually. Let us make a little chamber, I pray thee, on the wall; and let us set for him there a bed, and a table, and a stool, and a candlestick: and it shall be, when he cometh to us, that he shall turn in thither.

2 Kings 4:8-10 (KJV)

Whether or not we think of this woman as a leader among her people, we must agree that her quality of faith must be found in a leader of any worth.

God also used a certain woman of Thebez to save the city and all of its inhabitants as well as to deal with the wickedness of Abimelech. "And a certain woman cast a piece of a millstone upon Abimelech's head, and all to brake his skull" (Judg. 9:53 KJV). This woman was taking part in the defense of her city and had the courage to make hard decisions that would benefit her people and carry them out to their necessary conclusion. This is a requirement for any leader of worth.

Imagine the faith that was necessary for a woman like Jochebed to set her child to sail on the crocodile infested waters of a river where pagan worshipers cast their children as sacrifices to their gods. This daughter of Levi was the mother of Moses, deliverer of the Hebrews:

> And there went a man of the house of Levi, and took *to wife* a daughter of Levi. And the woman conceived, and bare a son: and when she saw him that he was a goodly child, she hid him three months. And when she could not longer hide him, she took for him an ark of bulrushes, and daubed it with slime and with pitch, and put the child therein; and she laid it in the flags by the river's brink. Exodus 2:1-3 (KJV)

She was then brought into Pharaoh's house and took part in the raising and training of this future leader.

When her father was torn by grief at the thought of fulfilling his vow to God, Jephthah bravely encouraged him to honor God at the expense of her own life. Her ready willingness to yield to the will of God can be compared to that of the virgin Mary who said, "be it unto me according to thy word" (Luke 1:38

KJV). And Jephthah said unto him, "My father, *if* thou hast opened thy mouth unto the LORD, do to me according to that which hath proceeded out of thy mouth; forasmuch as the LORD hath taken vengeance for thee of thine enemies, *even* of the children of Ammon" (Judg. 11:36 KJV). She considered the faithfulness of God should be honored by the faithfulness of His servants. This is not just a picture of humble submission to protect the honor of her father, but a courageous yielding to the way and will of God as an example for others.

She was not killed by her father, as some have portrayed, but was given to the life of a Nazarite and would therefore be a virgin for life.

And the LORD spake unto Moses, saying, Speak unto the children of Israel, and say unto them, When either man or woman shall separate *themselves* to vow a vow of a Nazarite, to separate *themselves* unto the LORD. Numbers 6:1-2 (KJV)

It is of interest here to note that, according to the record in Judges 13:1-24, the Angel of the Lord appeared to Hannah, Manoah's wife, mother of Samson, and spoke to her and not her husband. She was given instruction to "drink no wine or strong drink and eat nothing unclean." When she told her husband of her encounter with the Man of God, her husband Manoah called out to the Lord. This shows that he was a wise man who was not willing to raise the promised child without instruction from God. He was not only married to a godly woman, but a man that sought God and that God listened to.

In answer to Manoah's request, the Angel of the Lord appeared to his wife first and then she came and brought her husband into His Presence. He was assured that his wife had seen and received instructions from the Angel of the Lord and he was allowed to prepare a burnt offering unto the Lord. It would seem that Manoah was more curious than anything else. He even presumed to ask the angel of the Lord's name which was secret [wonderful (Isa. 9:6)].

Manoah was fearful of having seen the Lord while his wife knew the nature of God and recognized that the Lord had not come to kill but to bless. This whole story shows that Manoah did not have any spiritual insight apart from his wife's insightfulness. She was a woman whose story was noted in Scripture as having an important place of influence.

Abigail, wife of Nabal, was a wealthy woman "of good understanding" who was married to a man who "was rough and evil" (1 Sam. 25:3 KJV). She is a perfect example of how a person should live when they are in an unfortunate marriage. Her example of overcoming in difficult circumstances can be followed by all who are in similar situations. Thorough study of her life will give the believer the secrets to being more than a conqueror in Christ. F. B. Meyer said, "Never let the evil disposition of one's mate hinder the devotion and grace of the other. Never let the difficulties of your home lead you to abdicate your throne. Do not step down to the level of your circumstances, but lift them to your own high calling in Christ. 'Be not conformed . . . but be ye transformed'" (Rom. 12:1, 2 KJV).[86] Although Abigail was not standing in the office of a prophet, yet she did prophesy to David as recorded in 1 Samuel 25:28-30:

> I pray thee, forgive the trespass of thine handmaid: for the LORD will certainly make my lord a sure house; because my lord fighteth the battles of the LORD, and evil hath not been found in thee *all* thy days. Yet a man is risen to pursue thee, and to seek thy soul: but the soul of

my lord shall be bound in the bundle of life with the LORD thy God; and the souls of thine enemies, them shall he sling out, *as out* of the middle of a sling. And it shall come to pass, when the LORD shall have done to my lord according to all the good that he hath spoken concerning thee, and shall have appointed thee ruler over Israel. (KJV)

For her wisdom and faithfulness, the Lord delivered her out of her circumstance and brought her into the house of the future King David to be his wife. This is a beautiful picture of the deliverance and relationship that awaits those who abide faithful to the King of kings.

There were also the daughters of Heman, King David's seer. According to the record of Scripture, he had sons and daughters that served in the temple. "And God gave to Heman fourteen sons and three daughters. All these were under the hands of their father for song in the house of the Lord, with cymbals, psalteries, and harps, for the service of the house of God, according to the King's order to Asaph, Jeduthun and Heman" (1 Chron. 25:5-6 KJV). The Psalmist David also made mention of these, and possibly others: "The singers went before, the players on instruments followed after; among them were the damsels playing with timbrels" (Psa. 68:25 KJV).

In the midst of these women of note is one who stands out as an influential leader of her day. This wise woman lived in Abel, a city noted for the wisdom of its people who were sought after for counsel in difficult situations. "Then she spake, saying, They were wont to speak in old time, saying, They shall surely ask counsel at Abel: and so they ended the matter" (2 Sam. 20:18 KJV). Her story can be seen in 2 Samuel 20:13-22.

The story tells us that as Sheba, son of Bichri, fled Joab, he hid himself in the city of Abel of Beth-maacah. Joab had pursued him and set up a siege mound against the city and undermined the wall so that it would fall. It was during this time that this "mother in Israel" ascended the wall and cried out to Joab. She informed him that she stood in the office of Judge and was able to settle the matter. As can be seen, this woman was of such demeanor that Joab was disposed to listen to her. She pleaded the cause of her city and quickly devised a plan to save her city from destruction. She was not only able to convince Joab that she could provide him with what he wanted, Sheba, but was able, through her influence, to convince the people of the city to cut off the head of Sheba and cast it down to Joab. Through her influence she led her people to avert the total annihilation of the whole city. Joab then blew the trumpet to call off the attack and "they retired from the city, every man to his own home," their mission accomplished. This wise woman of position and authority had saved the day through her ability to influence both her attacker and those who abode with her.

No story captures my heart like the well known story of Ruth, the Moabitess, that is recorded in the Book of Ruth. Though it is not a story of leadership so much as it is of faithfulness and submission, much can be learned from this convert from paganism. As her life unfolds we find a woman of great faith, virtue, integrity, and character, qualities that every leader must possess. The "Proverbs Thirty-One Woman" describes her in detail. Let's consider her contribution to those who now are called by the name of Christian (little anointed ones) after Christ Jesus, the Savior of the world. This pagan woman made a choice to follow the God of Naomi and, therefore, to follow Naomi:

And she said, Behold, thy sister in law is

gone back unto her people, and unto her gods: return thou after thy sister in law. And Ruth said, Intreat me not to leave thee, *or* to return from following after thee: for whither thou goest, I will go; and where thou lodgest, I will lodge: thy people *shall be* my people, and thy God *[shall be]* my God: Where thou diest, will I die, and there will I be buried: the LORD do so to me, and more also, *if ought* but death part thee and me. Ruth 1:15-18 (AMP)

Ruth was an amazingly focused woman. One of her great attributes was that she was "steadfastly minded": "When she saw that she was stedfastly [alert and courageously] minded to go with her, then she left speaking unto her" (Ruth 1:18 KJV). This is the mind set that God requires of those who walk in faith. There is always a clear call to "choose you this day whom ye will serve;" and the Lord always wants to hear, "as for me and my house, we will serve the LORD" (Josh. 24:15 KJV). We can see this same challenge in 1 Kings 18:21 (KJV) as Elijah came before all the people, and said, "How long halt ye between two opinions? if the LORD be God, follow him." A leader must be a person of resolute mind.

Ruth chose to have Naomi as her mentor rather than a pagan from her own family or country. This showed great wisdom on her part in that Naomi had a mentor's heart: "Then Naomi her mother in-law said unto her, My daughter, shall I not seek rest for thee, that it may be well with thee?" (Ruth 3:1 KJV). Naomi took Ruth as a daughter and would not rest until Ruth had rest and was blessed. A leader knows how to choose a mentor that has more experience and knows more than they do.

Ruth was not only a woman of faith, she knew early in her walk with the God of Abraham, Isaac and Jacob, to speak words of faith: "And Ruth the Moabitess said unto Naomi, Let me now go to the field, and glean ears of corn after him in whose sight I shall find grace. And she said unto her, Go, my daughter" (Ruth 2:2 KJV). She was willing to put action with her faith. "Let me go glean," she said. We understand these principles from verses such as, "faith without works is dead" (Jas. 2:20; 2:26 KJV). She spoke favor with the one in whose field she would glean, "him in whose sight I shall find grace," and verified that the words of Proverbs 3:4 (KJV), "So shalt thou find favour and good understanding in the sight of God and man," and

Proverbs 12:2 (KJV), "A good man obtaineth favour of the LORD," hold true. Every one who desires to lead must have the ability to put action with faith.

This remarkable woman was also a woman with a strong work ethic. She put in a full days work and only took minimal breaks that were necessary. "And she said, I pray you, let me glean and gather after the reapers among the sheaves: so she came, and hath continued even from the morning until now, that she tarried a little in the house" (Ruth 2:7 KJV). This and her reputation for being a woman of great character made her the talk of the town and of great interest to Boaz. "And Boaz answered and said unto her, It hath fully been shewed me, all that thou hast done unto thy mother in law since the death of thine husband: and *how* thou hast left thy father and thy mother, and the land of thy nativity, and art come unto a people which thou knewest not heretofore" (Ruth 2:11 KJV). "And now, my daughter, fear not; I will do to thee all that thou requirest: for all the city of my people doth know that thou art a virtuous woman" (Ruth 3:11 KJV).

We can find the answer to Ruth's questioning of Boaz, "Why have I found grace in thine eyes, that thou shouldest take knowledge of me, seeing I *am* a stranger?" (Ruth 2:10 KJV), is that she was a woman of faith, integrity, and character. She got his attention by being an exceptionally virtuous woman. Faith, integrity, character, and the willingness to work is inseparable from the life of a leader.

The reward of faith spoken and acted upon with integrity and good character is a full reward. "The LORD recompense thy work, and a full reward be given thee of the LORD God of Israel, under whose wings thou art come to trust" (Ruth 2:12 KJV).

You and I must, like Ruth, learn to trust The Lord! Let our prayer be that of the Psalmist, "Keep me as the apple of the eye, hide me under the shadow of thy wings, How excellent *is* thy lovingkindness, O God! therefore the children of men put their trust under the shadow of thy wings" (Psalm 17:8; 36:7 KJV). Let our declaration be, "Because thou hast been my help, therefore in the shadow of thy wings will I rejoice" (Psalm 63:7 KJV), and let us rest in that, "He that dwelleth in the secret place of the most High shall abide under the shadow of the Almighty" (Psalm 91:1 KJV).

The "full reward" of Ruth was the Savior of the World as prophesied by the people and the Elders at the Gate:

And all the people that *were* in the gate, and the elders, said, *We are* witnesses. The LORD make the woman that is come into thine house like Rachel and like Leah, which two did build the house of Israel: and do thou worthily in Ephratah, and be famous in Bethlehem: And let thy house be like the house of Pharez, whom Tamar bare unto Judah, of the seed which the LORD shall give thee of this young woman. Ruth 4:11-12 (KJV)

Ruth, the Moabitess, was the great grandmother of King David and in the lineage of Jesus the Christ, our Savior. She was a type of the Church; the Gentile Bride to the Kinsman Redeemer! The "full reward" for her faith is seen in you, and in me! We are her seed by faith in Christ Jesus.

Let us, like Ruth, be a people of faith, integrity, and character. Let us, like Ruth, be a people who have learned to trust in the shadow of His wings to the point that His shadow and our shadow become one. "And he said, Who *art* thou? And she answered, I *am* Ruth thine handmaid: spread therefore thy skirt over thine handmaid; for thou art a near kinsman" (Ruth 3:9 KJV). I break into song at every remembrance of this powerful story, "Cover me, cover me. Extend the border of thy garment over me. Because thou art, my nearest Kinsman. Cover me, cover me, cover me."

May we become so one with Jesus, one with and in His Spirit, that it will be testified of us that they brought the sick into the streets, and laid them on beds and couches, that our shadow passing by might cover them and heal them (Acts 5:15).

The story of Job and his daughters is an interesting one. After coming through his difficult time, Job was blessed beyond measure as can be seen by reading the following:

So the Lord blessed the latter end of Job more than his beginning: for he had fourteen thousand sheep, and six thousand camels, and a thousand yoke of oxen, and a thousand she asses. He had also seven sons and three daughters. And he called the name of the first, Jemima; and the name of the second, Kezia; and the name of the third, Keren-happuch. And in all the land were no women found so fair as the daughters of Job: and their father gave them inheritance among their brethren. Job 42:12-15 (KJV)

I find it very interesting that his daughters' names were recorded though his sons were not. This gives them a special place in the notice of God and a prominence above their brothers. It is also of note that these young ladies received equal inheritance with their brothers. Culturally, this was not the norm though it can be seen several times in Scripture. Though there is no inference for, nor against, leadership ability in these young ladies, in instances of this type it clearly reveals that God does not regard gender when He purposes to bless people.

Lemuel the King had the benefit of a woman who was of exceptional make up. It was she whom we learn from in Proverbs 31:1-9. The wisdom of Lemuel's mother is a tribute to the ability of a woman to train a son, or any man for that matter. To even consider that a woman cannot teach a man anything is the height of conceit, which is nothing less than self-love expressed in excessive pride. Contrary to what many think, there never was a scriptural admonition against all women teaching all men. Q. M. Adams, referring to 1 Timothy 2:11, 12, points out that, "Paul refers not to women teaching men in general, but to wives abusing their influence over their husbands."[87]

As we discussed on pages 20 and 21, Paul was addressing how men and women should treat each other, especially in public. Mutual respect is the theme of the biblical record. We really need to take a thoughtful look at the context of the Scriptural record as it relates to era, custom, and circumstance.

Kelly Varner adds a new twist to our understanding of these verses when he notes:

> The phrase, "I suffer not a woman to teach
> . . ." appears to be timeless. But the verb in the
> Greek text is present, active indicative and thus
> reads, "I am not *presently permitting* a woman
> to teach . . ." Nero is dead. Go ahead and
> minister, ladies!
>
> Having noted that the gender of the soul is
> feminine, Paul was also saying, "Let the soul
> learn in silence with all subjection, for I do not
> allow the soul realm to teach, or usurp authority
> over the spirit realm, but to be in silence!"[88]

After reading the high commendation of the worth of a virtuous woman as portrayed in Proverbs 31:10-28, consider the verse 26 in the Amplified version of the Bible: "She opens her mouth in skillful and godly Wisdom, and on her tongue is the law of kindness [giving counsel and instruction]." Her spiritual Wisdom and ability to give counsel and instruction is the foundation of all of who she is. Again, the ability of a godly woman to counsel and teach is reinforced in the Old Testament Scriptures. By the way, this proverb has been set forth by some scholars as a model for the whole Church [The Bride of Christ] to follow and would be good counsel for any leader.

Let's not forget, Lydia, the "seller of purple". This astute and influential lady was a business woman who was of such influence that she led her whole house to the Lord. Her house then became a meeting placed for the church:

> One of those who listened to us was a woman named Lydia, from the city of Thyatira, a dealer in fabrics dyed in purple. She was [already] a worshiper of God, and the Lord opened her heart to pay attention to what was said by Paul. And when she was baptized along with her household, she earnestly entreated us, saying, If in your opinion I am one really convinced [that Jesus is the Messiah and the Author of salvation] and that I will be faithful to the Lord, come to my house and stay. And she

induced us [to do it]. Acts 16:14, 15 (AMP)

As the believers began to gather at her home one would allow that she would speak and teach there. There is no implication that a man was set over the gathering when Paul and Silas departed from there.

> And they went out of the prison, and entered into the house of Lydia and when they had seen the brethren, they comforted them, and departed. Acts 16:40 (KJV)

The attributes seen in these women may not set them apart as leaders, specifically, but they certainly do show qualifying attributes in each of them. Leaders, both male and female, must be those in who are developing the characteristics and inherent qualities that we have seen exercised in the life experience of these women of Scripture. While we may not find ourselves in their exact situations, we must recognize the qualities and strengths that allowed them to overcome their circumstances through their ability, and willingness, to think and act quickly in sometimes bold and creative ways.

End of Chapter Questions
Chapter IX

1. To what woman did the Angel of the Lord appear in Judges 13:1-24?

2. What woman's example can be followed by those found in unfortunate marriage situations?

3. Women, as well as men, served in the temple during King David's reign. This is found in what verses?

4. What woman is known for her great faith, virtue, integrity and character?

5. What qualities must be found in godly leaders irregardless of gender?

CHAPTER X – SUBMISSION

It would seem to be appropriate to consider the word "submission" here. I have lost count of the women who consent to the most vile situations and abuses and sincerely believe that no matter what a husband asks should be agreed to and pandered to for the sake of "being a submissive wife."

For instance, one woman I knew would go and sit in a bar and drink with her husband because he would tell her that if she were a good Christian she should submit to him and do what makes him happy. Another consented to all manner of sexual perversion because that is what her husband desired. She had been taught that she had to be a submitted wife and so complied with his pornographic fantasy inspired wishes. This is nothing less than doctrines of demons spoken of in 1 Timothy 4:1 (KJV): "Now the Spirit speaketh expressly, that in the latter times some shall depart from the faith, giving heed to seducing spirits, and doctrines of devils."

This is certainly not the intent of the eight occasions in seven verses that use the word υποτασσω, hupotasso, in the New Testament. Hupotasso is a Greek military term meaning "to arrange [troop divisions] in a military fashion under the command of a leader". In non-military use, it was "a voluntary attitude of giving in, cooperating, assuming responsibility, and carrying a burden". There is one verse, Hebrews 13:17, which uses the word υπεικω, hupeiko, and renders it "submit." This word means, to resist no longer, but to give way, yield (of combatants), or, metaphorically, to yield to authority and admonition, to submit. It carries the idea of one making themselves weak in the presence of another.

> Obey them that have the rule over you, and submit yourselves: for they watch for your souls, as they that must give account, that they may do it with joy, and not with grief: for that is unprofitable for you. Hebrews 13:17 (KJV)

The word "obey" is the word πειθω, peitho, and is used to mean, persuade, to persuade, i.e. to induce one by words to believe; to make friends of; to win one's favour, gain one's good will, or, to seek to win one, strive to please one; to be persuaded; to listen to, obey, yield to, comply with; or, to trust, have confidence, be confident. The two words "obey" and "submit" are working together to bring about an attitude of yielded confidence in those who are officially given "rule" [ηγεομαι hegeomai] over them, or more accurately, set as leaders before them.

The following verses contain the word υποτασσω, hupotasso: Romans 10:3, 1 Corinthians 16:16, Ephesians 5:21-22, Colossians 3:18, James 4:7, 1 Peter 2:13 and 1 Peter 5:5. Romans 10:3 and James 4:7, and are speaking of being submitted to God: "For they being ignorant of God's righteousness, and going about to establish their own righteousness, have not submitted themselves unto the righteousness of God." and "Submit yourselves therefore to God. Resist the devil, and he will flee from you." Timotheus and Stephanas were among those that, "have addicted themselves to the ministry of the saints" (1 Cor. 16:15 KJV), and were of such that Paul wrote, "That ye submit yourselves unto such, and to every one that helpeth with us, and laboureth" (1 Cor. 16:16 KJV). Over, and over again, we see a voluntary yielding to authority and admonition.

For us to consider that women can lead, we must understand verses like Colossians 3:18 (KJV), "Wives, submit yourselves unto your own husbands, as it is fit in the Lord." This cannot be done properly without considering it together with Ephesians 5:21-22 (KJV), "Submitting yourselves one to another in the fear of God. Wives, submit yourselves unto your own husbands, as unto the Lord." It is evident that the submission of wives to their husbands is within the context of those things that are "fit in the Lord." The word "fit," is ανηκω, <u>aneko,</u> and carries the understanding of submitting to that which is fitting or proper in the Lord. It must also be noted that this "submitting" is the same "submitting" that all Christians should do to one another. A verse that carries this thought out and expresses it a little bit differently is Philippians 2:3 (KJV) where we read, "Let nothing be done through strife or vainglory; but in lowliness of mind let each esteem others better than themselves." Each believer is to "esteem others better than themselves." This would cause them to "submit" to one another. The word "esteem" is ηγεομαι, <u>hegeomai,</u> which, as we mentioned previously, places others as "leaders before them." It calls for the same respect that one should have for the elderly. "Likewise, ye younger, submit yourselves unto the elder. Yea, all of you be subject one to another, and be clothed with humility: for God resisteth the proud, and giveth grace to the humble" (1 Pet. 5:5 KJV). The end of the matter is this, "Yea, all of you be subject one to another."

Most arguments for the superiority of the male and his position of ruler and covering over a woman seem to miss the great truth that "There are only two types of men [mankind] on planet Earth, Christ and Adam."[89]

On the same page as the previous quote we find Kelly Varner going on to say, and rightly so, that, "The Bible portrays these two kinds of hearts with a number of pictures - wheat and tares, sheep and goats, light and darkness, saints and sinners. Neither nature has any basis in gender, race or nationality."

Scriptures such as Ephesians 5:22 (KJV) and Colossians 3:18 (KJV), "Wives, submit yourselves unto your own husbands, as unto the Lord," and "Wives, submit yourselves unto your own husbands, as it is fit in the Lord," without proper understanding, are used as clubs to bludgeon women who don't know the heart of the Word of God as shown in the words "as unto the Lord" and "as it is fit in the Lord."

Granted, these precious women need to study the Word and prove what is the good, and acceptable, and perfect will of God. One thing is certain. Abigail had no problem doing what was right no matter what her husband said. That God was pleased with her demeanor and action was made evident when He delivered her out of her circumstance and into the loving care of David.

End of Chapter Questions
Chapter X

1. Define the Greek word, υποτασσω, *hupotasso.*

2. Define the Greek word, πειθω, *peitho.*

3. How do these two words relate to one another in our understanding of submissive obedience?

4. Define the Greek word, ανηκω, *aneko.*

5. Define the Greek word, ηγεομαι, *hegeomai.*

6. What two types of men [mankind] are there on planet earth?

CHAPTER XI – HUSBANDS

Consider with me, if you will, some women of influence whose husband's masculinity was not threatened by the greatness of their spouses:

From America's early days women like Harriet Beecher Stowe had a hand in shaping what it would become. Born into a prominent Christian family, her father was a well known minister who was involved in the anti-slavery movement. Her mother, Roxana Foote Beecher, prayed that the Lord would "put the call of service" in the hearts of her children, and that prayer was answered. After her marriage, Harriet lived near a slaveholding community and had contact with fugitive slaves. She learned the truth about their appalling existence and was <u>inspired by the Lord</u> to write a story about the evils of slavery. It was first published as a serial and later as the book *Uncle Toms Cabin*. Selling 300,000 copies the first year, it had a profound impact on public sentiment. Her book is credited with being instrumental in starting the Civil War and helping end slavery.

When she met Abraham Lincoln, he was said to have greeted her as "the little woman who made the book that made this great war."

Robert A. Corrigan in his introduction to a modern version of the book said, What makes *Uncle Tom's Cabin* decidedly different from much of the other important American fiction . . . is that goodness here is defined so absolutely in Christian terms.[90]

When women were viewed as second-class citizens, crusaders like Susan B. Anthony determined to change the world in which they lived. Although it is not widely known, Susan's Christian upbringing was at the heart of her mission to champion the cause of women's rights. Growing up she was taught and thoroughly believed that God is no respecter of persons and that He created all people equal, with no distinction between male, female, or race. However, Susan soon discovered that the world didn't share that view when she encountered the prejudice against women that existed at the time. It became apparent to her that if conditions were to improve for women, they needed the right to vote, and she took her place as a leader in the women's suffrage movement. She was a world changer.[91]

A woman by the name of Phoebe Palmer also made her mark on history with her husband along side. "Phoebe Palmer and her husband Walter stimulated the holiness movement through their lectures in the United States and Canada. Mrs. Palmer did most of the speaking and writing, and was also a leader in the early feminist movement."[92] Many were the men who followed her lead. "After Palmer, came a number of holiness leaders including Charles Parham of Topeka, Kansas; Charles Cullis of Boston; A.B. Simpson; and John Alexander Dowie."[93] According to Keith J. Hardman, author of Seasons of Refreshing, she was even credited with paving the way for the great revival in 1858. "The remarkable work of Phoebe Palmer prepared the way for the Revival of 1858." This Methodist lady "played an important role in stressing the experience of entire sanctification in Methodist circles." She also popularized the term, "Baptism of the Holy Ghost," as well as others.[94]

And what about the Sister Aimee Semple McPherson? "She was divorced," you may say. Yes, but from her writings, we can see that even through such trials she wrought many a wonderful work in the hands of the Lord. It was the men in her life that could not take the rigors of ministry.[95] She was indefatigable. "The holiness movement achieved fame during the 1920's through the ministry of Aimee Semple McPherson (1890-1944)."[96]

The late Fuschia Pickett, a great author and minister credited her husband as being a cut above most men:

> It takes a 'special man' of strength, security, and stamina to be the husband of a woman minister, teacher and writer. Leroy is that man. Though he does not speak publicly, he functions invaluably in our ministry, especially in the production of manuals, tapes and books. The message he preaches in the living of his life is one of total commitment to the mandate God has laid upon our lives. I am grateful to God for his love, encouragement and total support."[97]

I have always maintained that a man who knows who he is in Christ is not the least bit intimidated by anything, or anyone. He is free to encourage and support a woman in her calling without it hindering his calling or election in the slightest.

Here, I would not want to leave out "Catherine Booth (1829-1890), wife of William Booth and mother of eight children."[98] This woman not only kept her family in order but she helped establish the Christian Mission and the Salvation Army in 1861. According to Kelly Varner, in his book The Three Prejudices, this energetic and competent woman was considered to be the most popular preacher of her time.

Another great married woman of note is former Prime Minister of Great Britain, Margaret Thatcher. I remember being glued to the television set as the local Public Broadcasting station presented her life. Margaret Thatcher, Prime Minister of Great Britain, was not only a capable leader, but like Deborah of old, she held the esteem of the men with which she served the nation. She did not take her position as a platform to elevate women, but in fact preferred to work with men. This she did with great success. She was insightful, even prophetic, energetic, and capable beyond what many thought possible for a woman of state.

She was a married woman and was said to be very much a loving wife. According to PBS and the British Broadcasting Commission, her husband was a grand man who understood her call and was not threatened by it. He knew how to exert his influence to help her and supported her in whatever way she needed. He didn't need to be in front, known as her <u>head</u>, or any such thing. They worked together as a team even though she was the one with the call to rule a nation.

Dr. Paula Boyer, a woman with whom I have worked on the Southwest Regional Board of the Full Gospel Fellowship of Churches and Ministers, is another fine example of a married woman in ministry. Her husband, Victor Koozin, now retired, was a successful businessman who provides prayer support and great input into her life. He has never been intimidated by her being in ministry. He is her constant advisor in much of the day to day business of her busy life.

Joyce Meyers' teaching and traveling ministry could not function without the guidance and support of her husband, Dave. Both Marilyn Hickey and June Evans are married women with highly visible and successful ministries. Each of them are encouraged and supported by their husbands who are Pastors of their respective churches.

Denzil Hood is an astute businessman and an excellent administrator. This man of God is confident and always wears a heart warming smile. That he loves Jesus, no one can deny. He is married to Rebeca Hood, Pastor of Amigos de Fe [Friends of Faith] in Puebla, Mexico. This missionary couple is reaching the Mexican people by the thousands and was currently featured in G12 magazine. The article points out that their church numbers 6000 members and 800 cell groups.[99] The Gospel is shaking not only Puebla, Mexico, but Mexico City. Their ministry is also expanding into Central America and beyond because Denzil is not threatened by the tremendous anointing that is on his wife. She is a loving spouse, mother of three, and a powerful instrument in the hand of God as she pastors the people God has given her. These dear friends of mine are perfect examples of how a Priscilla-Aquila team might have looked.

My wife, Sharon, is a tremendous leader and minister of the Gospel. We are both strong-willed, opinionated individuals and don't always see things in the same way. This has done nothing but develop strength in each of us. We have learned greater appreciation for each other and are able to excel far beyond what either of us could without the other. Working together has allowed us to see our individual weaknesses and strengths and to allow the strengths of the other to enhance and strengthen the areas that are weaker. I have found that as I esteem and encourage her ministry, I become the better cared for, esteemed and encouraged. I have always maintained that if a man will treat his wife like a queen, she will treat him like a king. Fear is the one major thing that stops a man from encouraging his wife, or any other woman to excel in the things of God and the work of the ministry. Many are the powerfully anointed and gifted women whose call and gifting of God is nourished by unthreatened husbands that understand the ways of our Almighty Lord.

End of Chapter Questions
Chapter XI

1. The famous book, "Uncle Tom's Cabin," was written by whom?

2. What impact did that book have on the formation of the United States of America?

3. Who was Phoebe Palmer and what was she famous for?

4. Susan B. Anthony championed what cause?

5. Catherine Booth was considered to be what?

6. I have always maintained that if a man treats his wife like a _____ she will treat him like a king.

CHAPTER XII - TO THE JEW FIRST

Why didn't Jesus include women when He picked the twelve disciples? The answer lies within the context of Matthew 15:22-24. In Matthew 15:22 (KJV) we read:

> And, behold, a woman of Canaan came out of the same coasts, and cried unto him, saying, Have mercy on me, O Lord, thou Son of David; my daughter is grievously vexed with a devil. But he answered her not a word. And his disciples came and besought him, saying, Send her away; for she crieth after us. But he answered and said, I am not sent but unto the lost sheep of the house of Israel.

Jesus was sent to "The house of Israel" first:

> For I am not ashamed of the gospel of Christ: for it is the power of God unto salvation to every one that believeth; to the Jew first, and also to the Greek. Romans 1:16 (KJV)

To reach out to the Jew first dictated that those who were immediately around Him initially would be those accepted in the Jewish culture and religious society.

Even His initial commissioning of His disciples was to the Jew first:

> These twelve Jesus sent forth, and commanded them, saying, Go not into the way of the Gentiles, and into any city of the Samaritans enter ye not. Matthew 10:5 (KJV)

Again and again we can see that Jesus did everything possible to reach the Jew first. That this was well understood by His disciples is easily seen in these few following examples:

> And when they agreed not among themselves, they departed, after that Paul had spoken one word, Well spake the Holy Ghost by Esaias the prophet unto our fathers, Saying, Go unto this people, and say, Hearing ye shall hear, and shall not understand; and seeing ye shall see, and not perceive: For the heart of this people is waxed gross, and their ears are dull of hearing, and their eyes have they closed; lest they should see with their eyes, and hear with their ears, and understand with their heart, and should be converted, and I should heal them. Be it known therefore unto you, that the salvation of God is sent unto the Gentiles, and that they

will hear it. Acts 28:25-28 (KJV)

What then? are we better than they? No, in no wise: for we have before proved both Jews and Gentiles, that they are all under sin. Romans 3:9 (KJV)

I say then, Have they stumbled that they should fall? God forbid: but rather through their fall salvation is come unto the Gentiles, for to provoke them to jealousy. Romans 11:11 (KJV)

And he said, Go, and tell this people, Hear ye indeed, but understand not; and see ye indeed, but perceive not. Make the heart of this people fat, and make their ears heavy, and shut their eyes; lest they see with their eyes, and hear with their ears, and understand with their heart, and convert, and be healed. Isaiah 6:9, 10 (KJV)

But my people would not hearken to my voice; and Israel would *have* none of me. Ps. 81:11 (KJV)

For I would not, brethren, that ye should be ignorant of this mystery, lest ye should be wise in your own conceits; that blindness in part is happened to Israel, until the fulness of the Gentiles be come in. Romans 11:25 (KJV).

Once the Jews rejected Jesus as Messiah, the way was thrown open for the Gentiles to be gathered in; even as Scripture foretold:

And in that day there shall be a root of Jesse, which shall stand for an ensign of the people; to it shall the Gentiles seek: and his rest shall be glorious. Isaiah 11:10 (KJV)

I the LORD have called thee in righteousness, and will . . . give thee for a covenant of the people, for a light of the Gentiles. Isaiah 42:6 (KJV)

And he said, It is a light thing that thou shouldest be my servant to raise up the tribes of Jacob, and to restore the preserved of Israel: I will also give thee for a light to the Gentiles, that thou mayest be my salvation unto the end of the earth. Isaiah 49:6 (KJV)

Thus saith the Lord GOD, Behold, I will lift up mine hand to the Gentiles, and set up my standard to the people: and they shall bring thy sons in their arms, and thy daughters shall be carried upon their shoulders. Isaiah 49:22 (KJV)

And the Gentiles shall come to thy light, and kings to the brightness of thy rising. Isaiah 60:3

(KJV)

Jesus chose men, rather than women, to be the first Apostles to fulfill the Word of God that He would offer Himself and the Good News to the Jew first. After all, the initial messengers would not have been accepted at all if not male. The message had to be carried to the Jew in a manner acceptable to the Jewish mind-set of that time. Jewry was a male dominant society and a male dominant religious community; but Christ came to reconcile all unto God and the door was thrown open to all irrespective of any natural distinction.

It was their rejection of Him that opened the way for the Gentiles: "He came unto his own, and his own received him not" (John 1:11 KJV). "The Jews answered him, saying, For a good work we stone thee not; but for blasphemy; and because that thou, being a man, makest thyself God" (John 10:33 KJV). This can also be seen in Matthew 9:3 (KJV), "And, behold, certain of the scribes said within themselves, This man blasphemeth;" Matthew 26:65 (KJV), "Then the high priest rent his clothes, saying, He hath spoken blasphemy; what further need have we of witnesses? behold, now ye have heard his blasphemy." Mark 2:7 (KJV), "Why doth this man thus speak blasphemies?

who can forgive sins but God only?" Luke 5:21 (KJV), "And the scribes and the Pharisees began to reason, saying, Who is this which speaketh blasphemies? Who can forgive sins, but God alone?", and John 10:36 (KJV), "Say ye of him, whom the Father hath sanctified, and sent into the world, Thou blasphemest; because I said, I am the Son of God?"

Once Christ was rejected, then the glorious gospel was opened to the Gentiles, all were allowed to receive revelation, refreshing, nourishment, comfort, and strength from the Holy Spirit of God. All that pertained to God was now available to all irregardless of national origin, social status, or gender:

For by one Spirit are we all baptized into one body, whether we be Jews or Gentiles, whether we be bond or free; and have been all made to drink into one Spirit. 1 Corinthians 12:13 (KJV)

End of Chapter Questions
Chapter XII

1. Matthew 15:22-24 gives the reason for what?

2. What verse of Scripture states that Jesus had to go to the house of Israel first?

3. List, and review, the verses that show Jesus doing everything possible to reach the Jew first.

4. Once the Jews rejected Jesus as Messiah, the way was thrown open for the Gentiles. Give the Scriptures that show this.

CHAPTER XIII - NEITHER MALE NOR FEMALE

The obvious physical differences, coupled with intellectual and emotional differences of their basic nature, causes one to stop and ponder what can be meant by their being considered as the same by God.

It is widely accepted that men are primarily left-brain thinkers. This side of the brain processes thoughts: logically, sequentially, rationally, analytically, objectively, and tends toward random ideas. Women, on the other hand, are, generally considered to be right brain thinkers. The right side of the brain deals with things in an intuitive, holistic, synthesizing, subjective manner, and looks at wholes. Both men and women use both sides of their brains in varying degrees of prominence.

That the Lord did not sweep away all differences is obvious. So what differences were dissolved at the Cross? Could it be that our perception is clouded by the differences we see. God is not only reconciling all of mankind to Himself but is also reconciling one with another. The same picture is given as we consider that the Jews and Gentiles also needed to be reconciled. This is readily seen from texts such as Romans 10:12 (KJV) where we read, "For there is no difference between the Jew and the Greek: for the same Lord over all is rich unto all that call upon him."

Jews of that day ate different foods, danced different dances, enjoyed different jokes, and had a view of life that was entirely different than that of the Greeks. With this in mind we must realize that there must of necessity also be a reconciling of all distinctions for Christ to take His rightful place in our lives, societies, and cultures. "Where there is neither Greek nor Jew, circumcision nor uncircumcision, Barbarian, Scythian, bond nor free: but Christ is all, and in all" (Col. 3:11 KJV) is joined together with Galatians 3:28 (KJV) where women are included in the prejudice destroying work of Christ Jesus. All, not some, distinctions are put aside in Christ. Even those of gender: "There is neither Jew nor Greek, there is neither bond nor free, there is neither male nor female: for ye are all one in Christ Jesus."

This "all one," πας εις, pas heis, strongly emphasizes that the whole, everyone, all things, every-thing, collectively, some of all types, are in a relation of rest, εν, enone, in, by, and with Christ Jesus.[100]

As we can see, this is not a doing away with natural differences of culture, race, status, gender, etc. but a setting aside of stigma, prejudice and/or tradition that has arisen because of these natural differences. There is to be an appreciation for the perspectives, mannerisms, physical makeup, and bearing of others. The Kingdom of God has no place for distinctions that elevate or repress for any cause. With God all are regarded equally; all are met with the same degree of love, all are met with the same measure of grace. All are required to supply their unique giftings to the work of God. Ephesians 4:15, 16 teaches us that "every joint supplieth," not just those that are male. Every member of the Body of Christ is to offer their supply to the work:

> But speaking the truth in love, may grow up into him in all things, which is the head, even Christ: From whom the whole body fitly joined together and compacted by that which every joint supplieth, according to the effectual working in the measure of every part, maketh increase of the body unto the edifying of itself in love. Ephesians 4:15-16 (KJV)

We are no longer to consider, or regard, anyone

one after the flesh [earthly differences]:

> Wherefore henceforth know we no man after the flesh: yea, though we have known Christ after the flesh, yet now henceforth know we him no more. Therefore if any man be in Christ, he is a new creature: old things are passed away; behold, all things are become new. And all things are of God, who hath reconciled us to himself by Jesus Christ, and hath given to us the ministry of reconciliation; 2 Corinthians 5:16-18 (KJV)

Perhaps we should reach back into the Old Testament to see if there were any precedences of the grace of God extended to women along this line. The historical account of the daughters of Zelophehad comes to mind. Mahlah, Noah, Hoglah, Milcah and Tirzah came and stood before Moses, Eleazar the priest, the princes and all the congregation. They informed them that their father had died in the wilderness but that he was not involved with Korah's rebellion. Zelophehad had no sons and so they asked if they were not entitled to an inheritance. As Moses sought the Lord, the Lord said, "The daughters of Zelophehad speak right: thou shalt surely give them a possession of an inheritance among their father's brethren; and thou shalt cause the inheritance of their father to pass unto them" (Num. 27:7 KJV).

There is also the daughter of Caleb who married Othniel, son of Kenaz. She was as bold and strong as her new husband and had a good eye for business besides as can be seen by her bid for the water sources to go with the land. She easily received the blessing for which she asked:

And it came to pass, as she came *unto him,* .that she moved him to ask of her father a field: and she lighted off *her* ass; and Caleb said unto her, What wouldest thou? Who answered, Give me a blessing; for thou hast given me a south land; give me also springs of water. And he gave her the upper springs, and the nether springs. Joshua 15:18-19 (KJV)

Would God, our heavenly Father, be less apt to bless His daughters than Caleb? This would be a hard thing to believe when the Scripture clearly states that God considers his children above everyone, and everything, else:

Consider the ravens: for they neither sow nor reap; which neither have storehouse nor barn; and God feedeth them: how much more are ye better than the fowls? Luke 12:24 (KJV)

If then God so clothe the grass, which is to day in the field, and to morrow is cast into the oven; how much more *will he clothe* you, O ye of little faith? Luke 12:28 (KJV)

He is far superior in every way and gives much more in quantity and quality to his own. That this includes the spiritual graces that accompany the Holy Spirit is easily seen in Luke 11:13 (KJV), "If ye then, being evil, know how to give good gifts unto your children: how much more shall *your* heavenly Father give the Holy Spirit to them that ask him?"

End of Chapter Questions
Chapter XIII

1. What differences (between men and women) were swept away at the Cross?

2. What do the Greek words, πας εις, *pas heis*, teach us?

3. Ephesians 4:15 and 16 teach us what great truth?

4. We are to know each other in a realm other than the flesh. What realm?

5. Which Old Testament daughters received equal grace with sons?

CHAPTER XIV – CONCLUSIONS

It is true that experience should never be the final authority of faith and practice, but that Scripture must hold that high place, for it is God breathed.

> Every Scripture is God-breathed (given by His inspiration) and profitable for instruction, for reproof and conviction of sin, for correction of error and discipline in obedience, [and] for training in righteousness (in holy living, in conformity to God's will in thought, purpose, and action). 2 Timothy 3:16 (AMP)

Together, we have examined the scriptural record and taken note of its position on women in ministry, and women in general. As we join the biblical record together with experience, we gain a clear view of God's plan and purpose to use women in places of leadership, evangelism, teaching, and preaching. We need only to take a casual look at Church history to see that women played a vital role in spreading the glorious Gospel over the face of the earth.

It cannot be denied that in every great spiritual awakening, women were stirred by the Holy Spirit to pray, prophesy, teach, and preach in public assembly.

This was evident in the beginnings of the Society of Friends as it was so in the great evangelical revival associated with the names of Wesley and Whitefield. It has been so in that powerful renaissance of primitive Methodism known as the Salvation Army. The out pouring of the Spirit in Los Angeles called the Azusa Street Revival, under the leadership of Reverend William Seymour, was attended to by many women. Aimee Semple McPherson, Marie Wadsworth Etter, Clara Grace, Kathryn Khulman, and many others established denominations, held large tent meetings, conducted great crusades, while boldly proclaiming the Word of God to a lost and dying world. It has been increasingly so in this era of modern missions and modern evangelism in which we are living. Names like Gloria Copeland, Billye Brim, Marilyn Hickey, and Joyce Meyers are seen and heard daily on public television and radio. There can be no doubt to those with a hearing ear that these women are anointed, called and sent, preachers and teachers.

Let us take care how we regard women in ministry lest we find ourselves resisting the Holy Ghost even as the Pharisee Gamaliel warned the Council and the High Priest:

Then stood there up one in the council, a Pharisee, named Gamaliel, a doctor of the law, had in reputation among all the people, and commanded to put the apostles forth a little space; And said unto them, Ye men of Israel, take heed to yourselves what ye intend to do as touching these men. For before these days rose up Theudas, boasting himself to be somebody; to whom a number of men, about four hundred, joined themselves: who was slain; and all, as many as obeyed him, were scattered, and brought to nought. After this man rose up Judas of Galilee in the days of the taxing, and drew away much people after him: he also perished; and all, even as many as obeyed him, were dispersed. And now I say unto you, Refrain from these men, and let them alone: for if this counsel or this work be of men, it will come to nought: But if it be of God, ye cannot overthrow it; lest haply ye be found even to fight against God. Acts 5:34-39 (KJV)

Consider the following passages from the precious Word: "Quench not the Spirit. Despise not prophesying" (1 Thes. 5:19-20 KJV). The Holy Spirit gives gifts to whosoever He wills, without regard to gender, race, or ethnicity. The Lord was quite emphatic as He spoke the word to Peter which opened the door to the Gentiles, "And the voice spake unto him again the second time, What God hath cleansed, that call not thou common" (Act. 10:15 KJV).

It should be both a relief and a surprise to discover that there is no authority in the Word for repressing the witness of women in the public assembly, or for forbidding them to herald the glorious Gospel. What do you suppose could be accomplished if this tension could be removed from the framework of the Church?

The historically famous Edward Irving speaks very pointedly concerning the subject of women taking their place in the Body of Christ saying:

> Who am I that I should despise the gift of God, because it is in a woman whom the Holy Ghost despiseth not. That women have with men an equal distribution of spiritual gifts is not only manifest from the fact, but from the very word of the prophecy of Joel itself, which may well rebuke those vain and thoughtless people who make light of the Lord's work, because it

appeareth among women. I wish men would themselves be subject to the Word of God, before they lord so over women's equal rights in the great outpouring of the Spirit.[101]

Katherine Bushnell concludes her scholarly work and challenges all women with these words:

And what will the women of our day do? Will they say: "The prospect is too remote to be attractive to me. If I could see that by much effort, and by practicing a great deal of self-denial, anything could be accomplished worth while, *in my day*, the case would be different. But the little that I can do to hasten the evangelization of the world, and the coming of Christ will make no difference. I do not care to teach, or preach, or pray in public. I do not wish to be among those who are all the time proclaiming that Christ is coming again, and He never comes. They are a laughing-stock. I cannot join them." Such do not *"esteem the reproach of Christ greater riches than the treasures of Egypt."*[102]

Kenneth E. Hagin quotes Charles E. Robinson as saying:

I think you could say and prove that there are absolutely no Scriptural distinctions as to carrying on worship, or business either for that matter, which are based on sex. With God, there is neither male nor female, just folks. . . . The distinction God makes is not one founded in sex, but one founded in marital status.

In the same book, Brother Hagin then writes:

When it comes to the church - when it comes to spiritual things - when it comes to the body of Christ - there are no distinctions between men and women. As far as God is concerned, there are none. That's where many have missed it. They've made it a man-and-woman proposition - when it is not. It is a husband-and-wife proposition. The man is not the head of the woman in the church. The husband is the head of the wife in the home. "For ye are all the children of God by faith in Christ Jesus. For as many of you as have been baptized into Christ have put on Christ. There is neither Jew nor Greek, there is neither bond nor free, there is neither male nor female: for ye are all one in Christ Jesus" (Gal. 3:26-28 KJV).[103]

Charles Trombley ended his book with a simple, short and concise conclusion:

> In this study I've sought answers for the unanswered questions that are raised whenever women in active ministry are discussed, and I've shared those findings with you. My conclusion is this: nowhere does the Bible from Genesis to maps forbid any woman from serving God in any capacity He calls and prepares her to fulfill."[104]

Judy L. Brown writes, "God's perfect plan for women cannot be derived from the imperfection of the fall or of the law, but must be drawn from what is set forth in creation and from what is available again through redemption."[105]

After reviewing the Scriptures and the many excellently written and thought out books and papers on the subject of women in ministry, I cannot but come to the conclusion that women should be allowed every opportunity to follow the call of God on their lives. It is written that "One died for all . . . And that He died for all, that they which live should not henceforth live unto themselves, but unto Him which died for them, and rose again" (2 Cor. 5:14-15 KJV). All means all. Women must be allowed to live unto Him. The Bible clearly declares in Galatians 3:28 that there is no distinction between male and female in the eyes of God. If our Father does not consider the differences then neither should we.

It is my heartfelt desire that every member of the Body of Christ be liberated, equipped, and sent into the harvest fields. Jesus knew that this was the cry of the Father's heart. "Therefore said he unto them, The harvest truly is great, but the labourers are few: pray ye therefore the Lord of the harvest, that he would send forth labourers into his harvest" (Luke 10:2 KJV). Let us pray for laborers and then allow those who answer His call to fulfill His desire without regard to gender distinctions. Let the whole Body of Christ, every member in particular, take their rightful place in the economy and work of the Lord.

This book has only slightly touched on the many reasons our precious women should be allowed to move in the anointing and power of the call of God. Many are the scholarly works that can be found to give solid foundation for our consideration. You will find listed at the end of this dissertation, in the works cited list, some fine works that have been written on the subject of women in ministry. Prayerfully this will help you in your proper understanding of the Biblical basis for the placement of women in various positions of religious organization and church authority.

If you are a woman contemplating the ministry, be loosed from all constraints to pursue your destiny. Join the many women listed in the Full Gospel Fellowship of Churches & Ministries International directory.[106] This organization, among others, recognizes that the call of God is upon whom He wills.

If you are a man I encourage you to be supportive of any woman called of God. Together, let's go to the world with the glorious Gospel. Together, let's move in the power of Pentecost with signs following our preaching. Together, let us usher in the last great harvest and the return of the Great King!

End of Chapter Questions
Chapter XIV

1. Experience must always complement, and yield to, what high authority?

2. The Pharisee Gamaliel warned the Council and the High Priest against resisting the Holy Ghost in what verses?

3. Acts 10:15 teaches what?

4. What was Edward Irving's position on women in ministry?

5. The late Kenneth E. Hagin believed what about women in ministry?

6. What are we to pray concerning the harvest?

7. Is that prayer gender specific?

Appendix I

From an article penned circa 1890, concerning Acts 2:17-21, called <u>The Ministry of Women </u>by Adoniram Judson Gordon:

In order to reach a right understanding of this subject, it is necessary for us to be reminded that we are living in the dispensation of the Spirit - a dispensation which differs most radically from that of the law which preceded it. As the day of Pentecost ushered in this pristine economy which existed before the fall, so the prophecy of Joel, which Peter rehearsed on that day, outlined its great characteristic features. Let us briefly consider this prophecy.

Acts 2:17-21 "And it shall come to pass in the last days, saith God, I will pour out of my Spirit upon all flesh: and your sons and your daughters shall prophesy, and your young men shall see visions, and your old men shall dream dreams: And on my servants and on my handmaidens I will pour out in those days of my Spirit; and they shall prophesy: And I will shew wonders in heaven above, and signs in the earth beneath; blood, and fire, and vapour of smoke: The sun shall be turned into darkness, and the moon into blood, before that great and notable day of the Lord come: And it shall come to pass, *that* whosoever shall call on the name of the Lord shall be saved."

It will be observed that four classes are here named as being brought into equal privileges under the outpoured Spirit. 1. Jew and Gentile: All flesh seems to be equivalent to every one who or whosoever, named in the twenty-first verse. Paul expounds this phrase to mean both Jew and Gentile: For there is no difference between the Jew and the Greek.. For whosoever shall call upon the name of the Lord shall be saved (Rom. 10:12, 13). 2. Male and female: And your sons and your daughters shall prophesy. 3. Old and young: Your young men shall see visions, and your old men shall dream dreams. 4. Servants and Handmaidens: And on my servants and on my handmaidens I will pour out in those days of my Spirit; and they shall prophesy.

Now evidently these several classes are not

mentioned without a definite intention and significance; for Paul, in referring back to the great baptism through which the Church of the New Covenant was ushered in says: "For in one Spirit were we all baptized into one body, whether Jews or Greeks, whether bond or free" (1 Cor. 12:13). Here he enumerates two classes named in Joel's prophecy: and in another passage he mentions three: "for as many of you as were baptized into Christ did put on Christ; there can be neither Jew nor Greek; there can be neither bond nor free; there can be no male and female; for ye are all one man in Christ Jesus" (Gal. 3:28, R.V.).

We often hear this phrase, "neither male nor female," quoted as though it were rhetorical; but I insist that the inference is just, that if the Gentile came into vastly higher privileges under grace than under the law, so did the woman; for both are spoken of in the same category.

This is our starting point for discourse and the foundation from which I build the clear cut case for women in all levels of ministry. This prophecy of Joel, realized at Pentecost (Joel

2:28, 29; Acts 2:14 -18), is the Magna Charta of the Christian Church. It gives to woman a status in the Spirit hitherto unknown. And, as in civil legislation, no law can be enacted which conflicts with the constitution, so in Scripture we shall expect to find no text which denies to woman her divinely appointed rights in the New Dispensation.

"Your sons and your daughters shall prophesy." Here is woman's equal endorsement with man's for telling out the Gospel of the grace of God. So it would seem, for this word "prophesy" in the New Testament signifies not merely to foretell future events, and/or forth tell the Word of the Lord, but to communicate religious truth in general under a Divine inspiration,[107] and the Spirit of Prophecy was from now on to rest, not upon the favored few, but upon the many, without regard to nationality, class, or gender. What we see from the New Testament use of this word leads us to believe that it embraces that faithful witnessing for Christ, that fervent telling out of the Gospel under the impulse of the Holy Spirit, which was found in the early Church, and is found just as truly among the faithful today.

End Notes

1. King James Version / Amplified Bible Parallel Edition. (The Zondervan Corporation and the Lockman Foundation, 1995) (All Bible quotations will be taken from the King James Bible unless otherwise noted).

2. Charles Trombley, Who Said Women Can't Teach?: (South Plainfield, N.J.: Bridge Publishing, Inc., 1985) 1.

3. Samuel Pridequx Tregelles, Gesenius' Hebrew and Chaldee Lexicon. (Grand Rapids, MI: Baker Books, 1979) Strong's # 120

4. Loren Cunningham and David J. Hamilton, Why Not Women?. (Seattle, WA: Youth With A Mission Publishing, 2000) 14.

5. Cunningham, 15.

6. Joseph H. Thayer, Thayer's Greek-English Lexicon of the New Testament. (Grand Rapids, MI: Zondervan, 1968), # 2959.

7. George Barna, Leaders On Leadership. (Ventura, CA: Regal Books, 1997) 23.

8. Tregelles, # 7287

9.   J. Lee Grady, <u>10 Lies the Church Tells Women</u>. (Lake Mary, FL: Creation House, 2000) 71.

10.   Dr. Fuchsia Pickett, <u>God's Dream</u>. (Shippensburg, PA: Destiny Image Publishers, 1991) 94.

11.   Pickett, 96-97.

12.   Kelly Varner, <u>The Three Prejudices</u>. (Shippensburg, PA: Destiny Image Publishers, 1997) 102.

13.   Orr, J. Edwin. <u>Times of Refreshing,</u> London, England: Otter Creek Books, 1936

14.   Orr, 412.

15.   Thayer, # 4904.

16.   Charles L. Thompson, <u>Times of Refreshing, A History of American Revivals From 1740 to 1877</u>, (Chicago, IL: L.T. Palmer & Co, 1877) 412, 413.

17.   Thompson, 414.

18.   John MacArthur, <u>The Masters Plan for the Church</u>. (Chicago, IL: Moody Press, 1991) 94.

19.   Thayer, # 2271.

20. Eugene H. Peterson, <u>The Message: New Testament with Psalms and Proverbs</u>. (Colorado Springs: NavPress Publishing Group,1993)

21. Doriani, 9.

22. Alred Edersheim, <u>Sketch of Jewish Social Life</u>. (Grand Rapids, MI: Eerdmans, 1974)155.

23. Edersheim,155.

24. Edersheim,155.

25. Ken Ham, <u>Online Bible Greek Lexicon</u>. (Winterbourne, Ontario, Canada: Online Bible, 2003(# 1865.

26. Ham, # 1223, 32.

27. Grady, 129.

28. Pickett, 94.

29. Orr, 410.

30. Orr, 410.

31. Judy L. Brown, <u>Women Ministers According to Scripture</u>. (Kearney, NE: Morris Publishing, 1996) 269-270.

32. Thayer, # 306.

33. Leonard Swidler. <u>Biblical Affirmations of Women in Judaism</u>. (Philadelphia, PA: Westminster Press, 1979) 299.

34. Doriani, 9.

35. Keith J. Hardman, <u>Seasons of Refreshing</u>. (Grand Rapids, MI: Baker Books, 1994), 243.

36. Aimee Semple McPherson, <u>This is That</u>. (Los Angeles: Echo Park Evangelistic Association, Inc., 1923)

37. Tregelles, Strong's # 5031

38. Tregelles, Strong's # 3941.

39. John Maxwell, <u>The 21 Most Powerful Minutes in a Leaders Day</u>. (Georgia: Maxwell Motivation, Inc., 2000) 101.

40. Conner, 231

41. Varner, 39.

42. Conner, 231.

43. Conner, 246.

44. Conner, 253.

45. Roberts, 91.

46. Roberts, 85

47. Adams, 57

48. Adams, 58

49. King James Version / Amplified Bible Parallel Edition.

50. Thayer, # 1538.

51. Sidney I. Landau and Ronald J. Bogus, The Doubleday Dictionary. (Garden City, New York 1975) 572

52. Wayne A. Mack and David Swavely, <u>Life in the Father's House</u>. (Phillipsburg, NJ: R&R Publishing, 1996) 81.

53. Cunningham, 102

54. Cunningham, 103

55. Cunningham, 103

56. Cunningham, 103

57. Varner, 102

58. Pickett, 94

59. "Focus On The Family," James Dobson, KILA, June. 2003.

60. Stan Guthrie, <u>A Woman's Place In Missions</u>. (Location Unknown: Word Pulse) 28.

61. Herbert Lockyer, <u>All The Women Of The Bible</u>. (Grand Rapids, MI: Zondervan Publishing House, 1967) 13.

62. Guthrie, 28.

63. Guthrie, 28.

64. Ham, # 3408.

65. Doriani, 9.

66. Doriani, 9.

67. Doriani, 9.

68. Jackie Pullinger with Andrew Quicke, <u>Chasing The Dragon</u>. (Ann Arbor, MI: Servant Books, 1982)

69. Doriani, 9.

70. George Barna, (Barna Research Ltd., 2003) http://www.barna.org/cgi-bin/MainTrends.asp

71. Rev. B.T. Roberts, <u>Ordaining Women</u>. (Rochester, NY: Earnest Christian Publishing House, 1891) 125.

72. Roberts, 127.

73. Karen Adlong, "Women of Faith the Real World Changers," <u>Believer's Voice of Victory</u> May 2003: 26.

74. John C. Maxwell. <u>The 21 Irrefutable Laws of Leadership</u>. (Nashville, TN: Thomas Nelson Publishers, 1998) 68.

75. Peter Marshall and David Manuel, <u>The Light and the Glory</u>. (Old Tappan, NJ: Fleming H. Revel Company 1986) 285.

76. Varner, 78.

77. Maria Woodworth-Etter, <u>Diary of Signs and Wonders</u>. (Tulsa, OK: Harrison House, 1916) 79.

78. Graham Truscott, <u>What Does The Bible Teach About Women's Ministry?</u>. (Poona, India: New Life Centre, 1974) 19.

79. Truscott, 20.

80. Roberts, 129.

81. Peter Marshall with David Manuel. <u>From Sea to Shining Sea</u>. (Old Tappan, NJ: Fleming H. Revel Company, 1986) 219.

82. Maxwell, 68

83. Roberts Lairdon. <u>Kathryn Kuhlman.</u> (Tulsa, OK: Harrison House, 1990) 8, 9.

84. Katherine M. Haubert, <u>Women as Leaders</u>. (Monrovia, CA: MARC, 1993)

85. Lockyer, 70.

86. F. B. Meyer, <u>Moses</u>. (Fort Washington, PA: Christian Literature Crusade, 1984)

87. Q.M. Adams, <u>Neither Male Nor Female</u>. (Dallas, TX: Christ For The Nations, 1977) 168.

88. Varner, 99

89. Varner, 3.

90. Adlong, 27.

91. Adlong, 27.

92. Hardman, 169.

93. Hardman, 242.

94. Hardman, 242.

95. McPherson.

96. Hardman, 243.

97. Pickett, Dedication Page.

98. Varner, 78.

99. César Castellanos, G12 Spotlight on Success, Friends of Faith World Outreach. (G12 Harvest Magazine, North America, 2002) 7.

100. Thayer, # 3950; 1520.

101. Orr, 459.

102. Katherine Bushnell, God's Word to Women. (North Collins, NY: Ray Munson) 838.

103. Kenneth E. Hagin, The Woman Question. (Tulsa, OK: Manna Christian Outreach, 1975) 92-93.

104. Trombley, 231.

105. Brown, 16.

106. Jerry Hobbs, The Fellowship Directory 2003. (Dallas, TX: Full Gospel Fellowship of Churches and Ministries, 2003)

107. Orr, 49.

List of Works Cited

- Adams, Q.M., Neither Male Nor Female. Dallas, TX: Christ For The Nations, 1977
- Adlong, Karen. "Women of Faith the Real World Changers." Believer's Voice of Victory May 2003: 26-27
- Barna, George. Leaders On Leadership. Ventura, CA: Regal Books, 1997
- Barna Research Group Ltd., 2003 <http://www.barna.org/cgi-bin/ MainTrends.asp>
- Brown, Judy L. Women Ministers According to Scripture. Kearney, NE: Morris Publishing, 1996
- Bushnell, Katherine. God's Word to Women. North Collins, NY: Ray Munson
- Castellanos, César, G12 Spotlight on Success, Friends of Faith World Outreach. G12 Harvest Magazine North America, 2002
- Conner, Kevin J. The Church in the New Testament. Portland, OR: Bible Temple Publishing
- Cunningham, Loren and David J. Hamilton, with Janice Rogers. Why Not Women?. Seattle, WA: Youth With A Mission Publishing, 2000
- Doriani, Dan. "Women and Ministry: What the Bible Teaches," Current Thoughts and Trends (Colorado Springs, CO: August, 2003) 8-9.
- Edersheim, Alred. Sketch of Jewish Social Life. Grand Rapids, MI: Eerdmans, 1974
- Dobson, James. Focus On The Family. KILA 950 Radio, June, 2003
- Grady, J. Lee. 10 Lies the Church Tells Women. Lake Mary, FL: Creation House, 2000
- Guthrie, Stan. A Woman's Place in Missions. Unknown: World Pulse, 2000

- Hagin, Kenneth E. The Woman Question. Tulsa, OK: Manna Christian Outreach, 1975
- Ham, Ken. Online Bible Greek Lexicon. Winterbourne, Ontario, Canada: Online Bible, 2003
- Hardman, Keith J. Seasons of Refreshing. Grand Rapids, MI: Baker Books, 1994
- Haubert, Katherine M. Women as Leaders. Monrovia, CA: MARC, 1993
- Hobbs, Jerry. The Fellowship Directory 2003. Dallas, TX: Full Gospel Fellowship of Churches and Ministries, 2003
- King James Version / Amplified Bible Parallel Edition. The Zondervan Corporation and the Lockman Foundation, 1995
- Lairdon, Roberts. Kathryn Kuhlman. Tulsa, OK: Harrison House, 1990
- Landau, Sidney I. and Ronald J. Bogus, The Doubleday Dictionary. Garden City, New York, 1975
- Lockyer, Herbert. All The Women Of The Bible. Grand Rapids, MI: Zondervan Publishing House, 1967
- MacArthur, John. The Masters Plan for the Church. Chicago, IL: Moody Press, 1991
- McPherson, Aimee Semple. This is That. Los Angeles: Echo Park Evangelistic Association, Inc., 1923
- Mack, Wayne A. and David Swavely. Life in the Father's House. Phillipsburg, NJ: R&R Publishing, 1996
- Marshall, Peter, and David Manuel. The Light and the Glory. Old Tappan, NJ: Fleming H. Revel Company, 1986

- <u>From Sea to Shining Sea</u>. Old Tappan, NJ: Fleming H. Revel Company, 1986
- Maxwell, John C. <u>The 21 Irrefutable Laws of Leadership</u>. Nashville, TN: Thomas Nelson Publishers, 1998
- <u>The 21 Most Powerful Minutes in a Leaders Day</u>. Georgia: Maxwell Motivation, Inc., 2000
- Meyer, F. B. <u>Moses</u>. Fort Washington, PA: Christian Literature Crusade, 1984
- Peterson, Eugene H. <u>The Message: New Testament with Psalms and Proverbs</u>. Colorado Springs: NavPress Publishing Group,1993
- Pickett, Dr. Fuchsia. <u>God's Dream</u>. Shippensburg, PA: Destiny Image Publishers, 1991
- Pullinger, Jackie with Andrew Quicke. <u>Chasing the Dragon</u>. Ann Arbor, MI: Servant Books, 1982
- Orr, J. Edwin. <u>Times of Refreshing,</u> London, England: Otter Creek Books, 1936
- Roberts, Rev. B.T., <u>Ordaining Women</u>. Rochester, NY: Earnest Christian Publishing House, 1891
- Swidler, Leonard. <u>Biblical Affirmations of Women in Judaism</u>. Philadelphia, PA: Westminster Press, 1979
- Thayer, Joseph H. <u>Thayer's Greek-English Lexicon of the New Testament.</u> Grand Rapids, MI: Zondervan, 1968
- Thompson, Charles L. <u>Times of Refreshing, A History of American Revivals from 1740 t0 1877</u> , Chicago, IL: L.T. Palmer & Co, 1877
- Tregelles, Samuel Prideaux. <u>Gesenius' Hebrew and Chaldee Lexicon</u>. Grand Rapids, MI: Baker Book House, 1979
- Trombley, Charles. <u>Who Said Women Can't Teach?</u>: South Plainfield, N.J.: Bridge Publishing, Inc., 1985

- Truscott, Graham. <u>What Does The Bible Teach About Women's Ministry?</u>. Poona, India: New Life Centre, 1974
- Varner, Kelly. <u>The Three Prejudices</u>. Shippensburg, PA: Destiny Image Publishers, 1997

Other Resources

- Anderson, Leith. <u>A Church For The 21st Century</u>. Minneapolis, Minnesota: Bethany House Publishers, 1992
- Brooten, Bernadette J. <u>Women Leaders in the Ancient Synagogue</u>. Chico, CA: Scholars Press,1982
- Daily, Starr. <u>Love Can Open Prison Doors</u>. Great Britain: Purnell and Sons, Ltd., 1971
- Edwards, Jonathan. <u>Jonathan Edwards On Revival</u>. Carlisle, PA: The Banner of Truth Trust, 1995
- Ferrara, Jennifer and Wilson, Sarah Hinlicky. "Ordaining Women: two views," <u>Current Thoughts and Trends</u> (Colorado Springs, CO: August, 2003) 14.
- Hoppin, Ruth. "The Legacy of Katherine Bushnell." <u>Herstories</u> Unknown publication, 1985
- Meyer, F. B. <u>Through the Bible Day by Day</u>. Ft. Washington, PA: Christian Literature Crusade, 1979
- Piper, John and Grudem, Wayne. <u>Recovering Biblical Manhood & Womanhood</u>. Wheaton, IL: Crossway Books, 1991
- Shelley, Bruce L. <u>Church History In Plain Language</u>. Dallas, TX: Word Publishing, 1995
- Stertzer, Carol Chapman. "Hairpiece Revival." <u>Charisma</u> Mar. 2003: 28-31
- Strong, James. <u>Strong's Exhaustive Concordance</u>. Grand Rapids, MI: Baker Book House, 1977
- Waugh, Geoff. <u>Flashpoints of Revival</u>. Shippensburg, PA: Revival Press, 1998
- Woodworth-Etter, Maria. <u>Signs & Wonders</u>. Tulsa, OK: Harrison House, 1916

Other life changing books & brochures by the Author

Tongues, When &Why?
(also in Spanish)
Strongholds In The Mind
(also in Spanish)
Authority - The Centurion's Secret
What Now?
How To Win The Lost
Symbolism - Smoke & Mirrors in Modern Society
Halloween - History, Hype & Hyperbole
Christmas - Symbolism, Significance & Practice
Should A Woman be in The Ministry?

Books by Dr. Sharon H. Stover, R.N., D. Min., Th. D., Ph.D.

Fasting: a Guide
How to have a Personal Revival
The Person and Work of the Holy Spirit
The Serpent Within
John The Baptist
Gifts of the Holy Spirit
Fruit of the Holy Spirit
Husbands, Love Your Wives
God Will Turn Your Captivity
Seed of the Woman

Other Books, Booklets, Tapes & CDs by the Author
available at
http://www.smartcart.com/wellspring/index
.cgi?page=welcome.htm
or
Wellspring Bible & Book Store
P.O. Box 33418
Las Vegas, NV 89133-3418
702 631-5027 or WeCAN@CFaith.com

If you would like to have either, George and/or
Sharon speak and minister at your church or
organization, please contact:

Dr. George M. Stover Jr.
Wellspring Ministries
4870 Janell Drive
Las Vegas, NV 89149
(702) 631-5027 or WeCAN@CFaith.com

www.ingramcontent.com/pod-product-compliance
Lightning Source LLC
Chambersburg PA
CBHW031951080426
42735CB00007B/354